Klaus Baakes

# Key Issues of Syntax in the Special Languages of Science and Technology

## English – German

JULIUS GROOS VERLAG HEIDELBERG

Die Deutsche Bibliothek – CIP-Einheitsaufnahme

**Baakes, Klaus:**
Key Issues of Syntax in the Special Languages
of Science and Technology. English-German /
Klaus Baakes. – Heidelberg: Groos, 1994
ISBN 3-87276-706-2

ISBN 3-87276-706-2

Druck und buchbinderische Verarbeitung:
Difo-Druck GmbH, D-96052 Bamberg

## CONTENTS

**ABBREVIATIONS**

| | | |
|---|---|---|
| C | = | Complement |
| cf. | = | confer (Latin: compare) |
| ed. | = | editor |
| Eng. | = | Engineering |
| En | = | English |
| e.g. | = | exempli gratia (Latin: for example) |
| ESL | = | English Special Languages |
| ESP | = | English for Special Purposes |
| EST | = | English for Science and Technology |
| et al. | = | et alii (Latin: and others) |
| etc. | = | et cetera (Latin: and others; and so forth) |
| etw. | = | etwas (Ge: something) |
| f | = | following page |
| ff | = | following pages |
| FS | = | Fachsprache(n) (Ge: Special Language(s)) |
| GCE | = | A Grammar of Contemporary English |
| Ge | = | German |
| Ger. | = | Gerund |
| HTW/I (or II) | = | How Things Work, volume one (or volume two) |
| ibid. | = | ibidem (Latin: in the same place) |
| i.e. | = | id est (Latin: that is (to say); in other words) |
| Inf., inf. | = | Infinitive |
| LSP | = | Languages for Special Purposes |
| NP | = | noun phrase |
| NSE/I (or II) | = | VAN NOSTRAND'S Scientific Encyclopedia, volume one ( or volume two) |
| O, obj. | = | Object |
| OJE/8 | = | Oxford Junior Encyclopedia, volume 8 |
| O.m.I. | = | Objektskasus mit Infinitiv (Ge: object complementation by an infinitive clause) |
| P | = | Predicate |
| pp | = | pages |
| S | = | Subject |
| SE | = | Special English |
| SLST | = | Special Languages for Science and Technology |
| sth | = | something |

| | | |
|---|---|---|
| viz. | = | videlicet (Latin: namely) |
| vol | = | volume |
| VP | = | verb phrase |
| vs | = | versus |
| z.B. | = | zum Beispiel (Ge: for example) |

*Asterisked words or phrases should not be used.

# 1. INTRODUCTION

## 1.1 English for Special Purposes (ESP) and Special Languages

ESP is a relatively young branch of Applied Linguistics which is concerned with the study of the English usage in situations and spheres of communication that are scientifically, technically, economically, academically, or professionally determined. Its province, therefore, are the special languages (in Ge Fachsprachen) as used by specialists (scientists and engineers) in writing and speaking about their subject matter, such as the language used in Electrical Engineering or Nuclear Physics. Conceptually, the language-related term ESP is closely associated with its unspecified superordinate term Language for Special Purposes (LSP), which can be defined as a complete set of linguistic phenomena comprising terminological, syntactic, and stylistic features which are different from ordinary language and occur within a definite sphere of communication as indicated above (cf. also Hoffmann 1979).

In teaching ESP, every effort must be made to provide for a demanding language course or programme of instruction in which the content and the aim of the course are fixed by the specific needs of a particular group of learners. In tertiary education, i.e. at university and college level, for example, the ESP-needs of students of engineering or economic disciplines can be met by courses such as English for Mechanical Engineers, English for Electrical Engineers, Business English and Communication for Managers respectively. It should be noted, however, that both the authors of ESP-textbooks and lecturers in ESP stress the necessity for students to have a good command of English, preferably A level (General Certificate of Education Advanced Level), because it is (or should become) common practice to hold ESP-courses in English, in which students are expected to work on their own, playing an active part in dealing with relevant questions and problems in the field of ESP. There are plausible reasons for this requirement which are based on didactic and methodological considerations in the process of teaching subject-specific communication and enabling students to communicate their specialist knowledge in a professional setting efficiently and effectively (cf. Baakes 1992).

The expansion of ESP during the last two decades is due to new demands and requirements of the rapidly changing world of science, technology, and business as well as the challenges of the growing European Union. It is also due to what Kennedy/ Bolitho (1984, 1) have pinpointed as follows: "The importance of English as an international language continues to increase as more people are wanting or being required to learn English. For example, governments are introducing programmes with English as the first, and sometimes only, foreign language; the growth of business and increased occupational mobility is resulting in a need for English as a common medium of communication; and access to much scientific and technical literature is difficult for those with no knowledge of English."

It is interesting to note that English has also become an object of concern in parts of the English-speaking world in terms of an increasing awareness of the importance of technical communication for scientists and engineers as native speakers of English. Huckin/Olsen (1983, 3), for example, ask the question why scientists and engineers should study technical writing and speaking. Part of their straight answer is: "Scientists and engineers may be technically brilliant, and creative, but unless they can convince coworkers and supervisors of their worth, the technical skills will be unnoticed, unappreciated, and unused. In a word, if technical people cannot communicate to others what they are doing, and why it is important, it is they and their excellent *technical* skills that will be superfluous. From this perspective, communication skills are not just handy; they are critical tools for success, even survival, in 'real-world' environments."

## 1.2 Dominant Characteristics of English Special Languages

Among experts in the field of English Special Languages there has been broad consensus of opinion on the issue of what constitutes Special English (hereafter called **SE**), as opposed to 'general' English, ever since English Special Languages (**ESL**) became the subject of linguistic research (e.g. Strevens 1973, Sager et al. 1980, Hoffmann 1987). **SE** occurs in both written and spoken forms, although the former doubtless provide the extensive material that permits easy access to linguistic research and description and, therefore, are conventionally referred to when speaking of **ESL**.

Scientists and engineers are trained to be objective and to accept as facts only impersonal, objective statements about things which can be seen by any observers who choose to look. This objective attitude is naturally reflected in the way they express themselves and particularly in the kinds of syntactic structures and sentence patterns, which in terms of complexity, frequency, and distribution very much deviate from usage in, say, colloquial English or English prose.

In their work scientists and engineers aim at communicating primarily with other scientists and engineers. Normally, they do not need to make the subject they are dealing with seem interesting or exciting, since they are writing or speaking to those who have chosen to read or listen. So their way of saying things usually lacks variety. They are far more concerned with being accurate and concise, and they want to avoid any sort of misunderstanding. From all this it follows that the style of scientific writing is highly formal. The important feature of *formality*, surprisingly, is also common in spoken communication, i.e. as soon as a scientist or engineer is dealing with technical matters or discussing his own subject he naturally adopts the written forms of **SE**, tending to 'speak like a book'.

"But of course a scientist is also a social person. So you will hear scientists speaking personally and informally when they are being sociable, and impersonally and more formally when they are being scientific. The contrasts between these two styles illustrate how the English of science and technology differs from English of literature and everyday life" (Brookes 1971, 129).

The habits of thought that have been described so far lead to what is generally characterized as *objectivity*, *absence of expressiveness* and *emotion*, *precision*, *economy*, *conciseness*, and *formality* in the use of language in contexts which are usually about things, processes, properties specific to science, technology, or technical work. This necessarily results in recurrent grammatical patterns of ESL, which are predictable with fair certainty. Strevens (1973), however, points out that, although the scientist or engineer as educated native speaker of English is not, as a rule, consciously aware of them, he is very sensitive to grammatical features such as:

- sentence length (i.e. the number of clauses contained in sentences);
- type and sequence of clauses within a sentence, relative frequency of main and subordinate clauses;

- order of the subject in relation to the main verb, and the amount of variation in this sequence;
- number of adjuncts, i.e. adverbial and prepositional phrases, and their location initially or finally in the clause;
- relative frequency of particular verb forms (e.g. passive or active, tense, aspect, etc.);
- reference forward or backward in the text.

Strevens also refers to certain concepts which are common to all advanced and complex thought, no matter what the subject, and argues that these general concepts are expressed in English by the use of items such as **although, because, if, unless, until, whenever**, etc. He stresses that the scientist who cannot handle items of this kind, together with grammatical features such as *subordination, relativisation, co-ordination* in English cannot handle science in English; but he cannot handle any other discipline, either. He goes on evaluating the importance of these general concepts by saying that they state the logic - the rhetoric, the argument - of the text, as well as having grammatical consequences in that they do not fit into any single grammatical category and, for that reason, suggests to call them logico-grammatical items.

He distinguishes seven *notional* classes into which these items can be grouped according to the *notions* they convey and presents them with three exponents in each class for the purpose of illustration as follows:

- *linking* and *logical sequence of ideas,*

  **furthermore, thus, in addition to ...;**
- *paraphrase and apposition*

  **like, similarly, as if ...;**
- *causality*

  **because, therefore, as a result of ...;**
- *opposition or contrast*

  **however, nevertheless, in spite of ...;**
- *restriction*

  **except, unless, only if ...;**

- *hypothesis*

  **conclude, refute, suppose...;**

- *enquiry*

  **how big, long, many?, with what purpose?, to what extent?**

Hoffmann (1987) exemplifies the devices of **premodification** and **postmodification,** such as the frequent use of non-finites (e.g. gerunds and participles), verbless clauses, and adjectival clauses and discusses general features of ESL, which have been ascertained by linguistic analyses of sentences considered as entire structural units of scientific writing. These features include:

- a relatively long sentence length as a result of the complex sentence structure in scientific writing;
- as a consequence of the foregoing a greater number of clauses in sentences of scientific writing;
- the tendency to prefer reduced constructions of the number of those sentence patterns most frequently used in scientific writing;
- the prevailing use of declarative sentences in accordance with the strong informative intention of Special English;
- the greater amount of imperative sentences in technical than in scientific texts because "they are the normal method of expressing instructions, as in the assembly, dismantling or operation of machinery" (Sager et al. 1980, 202);
- the extensive use of relative and adverbial clauses in complex sentences where simple modifiers do not warrant the required precision, and adverbial clauses (of *manner, condition, cause, place,* and *time*) exceed adverbs and adverbials in exactness and clarity.

Sager et al.(1980, 219) highlight the dominating role of **nominal groups** in sentences of scientific and technical writing and show how the presence of this type of groups contributes largely to distinguishing **SE** from general English. "The most important components of the vast majority of **SE** sentences are conceptual units expressed in nominal groups. They contain the individual items of information which make up the detailed description of a machine or process, the logical exposition of an idea or theory, the reasoned explanation of natural phenomena and the objective evaluation of experimental data. They act as the building blocks from which **SE** sentences are constructed because they possess certain inherent qualities which enable them to perform the task of communicating information effectively and efficiently, namely

1. they can be placed as subject or object and then emphatically within syntactic constraint at the beginning or end of the sentence according to their relative importance;
2. they can be combined by means of structural words such as connective verbs, conjunctions, prepositions and relative pronouns;
3. their information content can be expanded by the insertion of different types of modifiers.

The possibilities of combining, extending and sequencing nominal groups available to the specialist writer are limited only by the ability of the intended recipient easily to comprehend the resultant text. In short, nominal groups are the most appropriate vehicles of condensed linguistic expression for scientists and technologists who are trained to perceive and consequently to speak about the physical world in terms of concepts, processes and quantifiable units. Their preference for nominal formulation as a means of information loading leads to the use of nominal groups, non-finite verbs and verbless clauses instead of finite verbs, where the latter might well be expected in other forms of English." This line of reasoning is very important and should be kept in mind because it suggests why the study of **clause-reducing devices** will be the primary concern of this book.

### 1.3 The Coverage of Distinctive Syntactic Features in ESP Books

In the field of **SE** systematic approaches to the study of syntactic structures of sentences with varying linguistic and didactic objectives date back to the mid-sixties when Herbert (1965) published his pioneering work 'The Structure of Technical English', which Swales (1985, 17) calls **"the first 'real' ESP textbook"**. This book which is based on an investigation into the characteristics of English found in scientific and engineering texts covers the structure of sentences rather than the text structures of scientific or engineering passages. According to Herbert's Preface "this practice book is intended for foreign engineers or students of engineering who have already mastered the elements of English, and who now want to use their knowledge of the language to read books on their own subjects." The reading sections have been specially written by the author, in consultation with colleagues from various engineering disciplines, with the aim "to illustrate features of technical style, and for no other purpose."

The research paper 'Wichtige syntaktische Erscheinungen im technischen Englisch' (Baakes 1967) brings the complex issues of the non-finites into focus. - Experience of teaching the subject of ESP to German students at tertiary level has shown that the non-finite forms of the verb, which occur on their own only in dependent clauses, and lack tense and mood contrasts, still pose major problems for the understanding of **SE** literature. The non-finites and related structures have therefore been studied in greater detail with the object of providing help and guidance on problems of **SE** syntax and usage for ESP students (see also section **1.5)**, as will be shown in this book.

Gerbert (1970) chose to cover everything peculiar to the syntax of **SE** in his treatise 'Besonderheiten der Syntax in der technischen Fachsprache des Englischen', which is an important contribution to the theory of a **SE** syntax (cf. Beier 1980, 54; Tinnefeld 1991, 16).

In his book 'Writing Scientific English' (1971) Swales gives practice in a series of structured contexts through which, he argues in the Preface, "foreign students of physical sciences and engineering can develop their ability to express their scientific and technical knowledge in English." The scope of this practice book includes the attempt to isolate the main grammatical difficulties likely to be encountered in descriptive work.

The article 'Grammar and Technical English' (Lackstrom et al. 1972) is discussed as one of the 'Episodes in ESP' by Swales (1985). It is concerned with four areas of English grammar as used in technical and scientific writing - tenses, the article system, the role of 'real' passives and statives, and the occurrence of nominalizations as opposed to passives.

Sager et al. (1980) give a full account of **SE** syntax under the heading 'The syntagmatic level' whereas Trimble in his practice book 'English for Science and Technology' (1985) presents a *rhetorical-functional* approach to EST discourse which focuses on the role of *functions* such as *description*, *definition*, *classification*, etc. as fundamental parts of the organization of scientific and technical information. He therefore does not refer "to the basic grammar of the English language but to those specific grammatical elements that appear to stand in a special relationship with some of the rhetorical concepts" (1985, 114).

Similar to Trimble's approach many authors of ESP practice books place great emphasis on *notions* and *functions* (e.g. Glendinning 1973 and 1980; Mullen/Brown 1984; Yates/Fitzpatrick 1988) while those syntactic constructions in **SE** that are difficult for foreign students to grasp, in particular the non-finites, are not given the attention expected by students of science and technology. Even in special books designed to describe the fundamental principles of ESP didactics and methodology (e.g. Kennedy/Bolitho 1984; Hutchinson/Waters 1987) the subject of **SE** syntax is outside the scope of the authors´considerations. It goes without saying, however, that at the advanced level of ESP the needs of students include **SE** grammar tuition directed towards the analysis of sentences - of parsing - so that students can understand the structure of the sentences they encounter in the perusal of English publications on topics of their special field of study. Parsing, as Leech (1988, 13) emphasizes, "is not an end in itself, but a means towards broader educational goals, which require us to see grammar as a central component in the processes of composing and understanding text and discourse."

The discrepancy between well-founded research results in **SE** syntax and the poor reflection of these results in ESP literature may be due to the shift of the focus on language at the sentence level to the level above the sentence, i.e. to larger units of language such as the paragraph, in the emerging field of discourse and rhetorical analysis, in which ESP became largely involved. This process necessarily resulted in abandoning, for example, special syntactic devices in sentence structures as research objects and attaching too much attention to *functions* and *notions*.

The underrated role of **SE** syntax in ESP referred to above is reminiscent of Beier's complaint (1980, 55) about the neglection of research into syntactic phenomena of **SE**: "Insgesamt gesehen sind in der Literatur zur FS insbesondere des Englischen Fragen der Syntax lange vernachlässigt worden... Wie selten eingehende Analysen sind, wird augenfällig durch den vergleichsweise geringen Raum demonstriert, den syntaktische Probleme in den Einführungen Flucks und Hoffmanns (1976) einnehmen."

It appears that this situation has not essentially changed since then, although there is certainly some scope for further research projects in this area as much as having improvement in the field of grammar in general English, as Bald (1988,3) remarks: "I am convinced that...numerous problems for teachers arise from a deficient grammatical analysis on the part of grammarians, sometimes linked with an inadequate terminology...". Bald (1988, 1) also holds the view that there are signs of grammatical prosperity - and there I completely agree with him - which he interpretes as being "indicative of a continuing need for grammatical instruction - whatever the type of course and whatever the educational philosophy behind it may be. Books, articles, in-service training courses, etc., confirm that the role of grammar is being reconsidered, and it seems that different educational factions are now prepared to admit that communication and grammar are not necessarily opposites but can rather be turned into allies on the way to a better command of English."

### 1.4 The Crucial Issue of the '-ing Form'

Few linguistic items have been the subject of such a highly controversial discussion as the **'-ing form'**, which ultimately resulted in the abandoning of the traditional distinction between the **'gerund'** and the **'present participle'** as structurally and functionally different uses of words ending in '-ing', a position held, for example, in the grammar books 'A Grammar of Contemporary English' (Quirk et al. 1972, 133-135) and 'A Comprehensive Grammar of the English Language' (Quirk et al. 1985, 1290-1292). Whether this position has helped to facilitate the treatment of '-ing structures' in grammar, thus supporting the teaching and learning process in English as a foreign language, is arguable. The terminological insecurity in the following quotation is a case in point: "You often want to refer to an action, activity, or process in a general way. When you do, you can use a noun which has the same form as the **present participle** of a verb.

These nouns are called different things in different grammars: **gerunds, verbal nouns, or '-ing' forms.** In this grammar we call them **'-ing' nouns."** Moreover, the reader learns: "It is sometimes difficult to distinguish an **'ing' noun** from a **present participle,** and it is usually not necessary to do so" (Sinclair 1990, 23). Both from an intralingual and interlingual point of view, based on the necessity of considering structural, functional, and semantic criteria, the suggestion that it is usually not necessary to distinguish an 'ing' noun from a present participle is not comprehensible at all.

This development and its resultant vagueness in treating the matter at issue has been commented with some pointed references by Lamprecht (1983, 138): "Offenbar aus Respekt vor der Tradition des Faches hat man sich lange bemüht, die Definitionen von Gerundium und Partizip, wie sie die Lateingrammatik formuliert hatte, auf das moderne Engl. zu übertragen. Anstatt die traditionellen Definitionen unvoreingenommen auf ihre Angemessenheit für das Engl. entsprechend den modernen linguistischen Erkenntnissen zu überprüfen und zu präzisierenden Neudefinitionen zu gelangen, hat man sich weitgehend zu einem die strukturellen Varianten nicht berücksichtigenden einheitlichen Terminus für alle ING-Strukturen entschieden, der augenscheinlich als bloßer 'Aufkleber' ('label') zu verstehen ist, indem man sie entweder insgesamt als 'Participle' oder aber insgesamt als 'Gerund' bezeichnet. Dabei hat man auch davon abgesehen, diesem terminologischen Notbehelf eine angemessene Motivierung mitzugeben, wie sie an sich durchaus möglich wäre."

There are other scholars who voice their criticism as well. Kirsten (1980, 48ff) takes up the problem of classifying '**-ing forms**' and argues as follows: "In ihrer monumentalen 'Grammar of Contemporary English' (GCE) lassen R. QUIRK et al. die Unterscheidung zwischen Gerundium und Partizip unberücksichtigt und unterteilen die 'words in -ing' lediglich in **deverbal nouns, verbal nouns** und **participles,** fassen also all das, was nicht **deverbal noun** und **verbal noun** ist, unter **participle** zusammen. Mit 15 abgestuften Beispielen veranschaulichen sie eindrucksvoll die unterschiedlichen Verwendungsweisen der '-ing-Formen' vom eindeutigen Substantiv **(deverbal noun)** in (1) *Some paintings of Brown's* bis zum eindeutigen Partizip innerhalb der erweiterten Form in (15) He *is painting his daughter.* Die Aufhebung der Unterscheidung begründen sie anschließend wie folgt:

'...the traditional view held *painting* to be gerund in

*Painting* a child is difficult

where the item is in a structure functioning nominally (in this case a subject), but it was considered a participle if the same structure functioned adverbially as in

*Painting* a child, I quite forgot the time.

No such categorial distinction, however, was made between

*To paint* a child is pleasant and

*To paint* a child, I bought a new canvas

where the italicized item was traditionally regarded as an 'infinitive' in both.

In this book we shall disregard the distinction between gerund and participle, classing the '-ing items' in (6 - 15) as **PARTICIPLES'.**" Kirsten points out that "Die Argumentation von QUIRK et al. beruht auf der Gegenüberstellung von **nominal function** und **adverbial function,** was sogleich ihren schwachen Punkt bloßlegt: die nicht genügend scharfe Differenzierung zwischen Struktur (z.B. Nominalphrase, Verbalphrase, Adverbialphrase) und Funktion (z.B. Subjekt, Objekt, adverbiale Bestimmung). **Nominal function** und **adverbial function** im Sinne der GCE schließen einander nicht aus, denn Nominalphrasen (NPs) treten massenweise in **adverbial function** auf,... Die Gegenüberstellung von **nominal function** und **adverbial function** und der Hinweis auf entsprechende Infinitivkonstruktionen sind damit als Argumente für eine Aufhebung der Unterscheidung von Gerundium und Partizip untauglich."

He finally makes a thorough analysis of the syntactic functions of '**-ing forms**' based on the assumption that '**-ing forms**' are reductions in terms of transitions from the unit of 'sentence' to the unit of 'word', i.e. from propositional to lexical nomination, and shows that '**-ing-forms**' occur in the same syntactic functions or positions as noun phrases. This is his conclusion: "Es ist demnach nicht einfach Haarspalterei, die für den Übergang von der propositiven zur lexikalischen Nomination im Englischen so bedeutsamen '-ing Fügungen' in Gerundien und Partizipien zu unterteilen. Was wäre auch gewonnen, wenn man *painting* in syntaktisch und semantisch so unterschiedlichen Äußerungen wie *He is painting his daughter* und *His hobby is painting his daughter* undifferenziert als Partizip bezeichnete. Qui bene distinguit, bene docet."

In Part I of his article '-ING' Matthews (1987, 136ff) investigates the status of the term '**-ing form**' vis-a-vis terms like '**participle**' and '**gerund**'. He comes straight away to the point by stating: "The traditional distinction, influenced by Latinate grammar, is between a participle, semidefined as a 'verbal adjective', and a gerund, semi-defined as a 'verbal noun'.

In view of a number of difficulties of assignment within the area of complementation, many grammarians, particularly pedagogical grammarians, proposed and established a label for what looks like one morphological element: the '**-ing form**'. I wish to argue against this position...". He does so convincingly in reviewing four selected discussions of the topic among which there is 'A Comprehensive Grammar of the English Language' (Quirk et al. 1985). Like Kirsten, he argues against their position to adopt the term '**-ing form**' and to justify this decision (ibid. 1292) by suggesting that if an alternative term is required **'participle'** might be generalized. Matthews particularly criticizes 'the rather weak reasoning' of their justification.

In his review he also includes Huddleston's 'Introduction to the Grammar of English' (1984) in which the distinction between **gerunds** and **present participles** is maintained, as is evident from the following: "Like a gerund, a present participle contains (at least) a verb stem and the suffix **-ing.** But whereas a gerund or, as we have preferred to put it, the phrase headed by a gerund, has nominal properties, a present participle, or again the phrase headed by one, allegedly has adjectival properties", a view which is also held by the two Eckersleys in their book 'A Comprehensive English Grammar' (1960, 237f). The definition of the **present participle** as having 'adjectival properties' is seen by Matthews as problematic. It is not accepted by Lamprecht (ibid. 139): "Auf keinen Fall zu akzeptieren ist allerdings die ... Definition des englischen Partizips als eine zwischen Verb und Adjektiv stehende infinite Form."

Some of Matthews´ conclusions from his review are very interesting and highly informative in that

- arguments for the categorial distinction between **gerund** and **present participle** outweigh;
- there are, nevertheless, difficulties of a categorial nature as to where one draws the line between nominal and adjectival or between adjectival and verbal;
- there are difficulties of assignment when the structural analysis is uncertain.

Until now the focus has been on the identical forms of **gerund** and **present participle**. Mention must be made, however, that the **gerund,** depending on its syntactic function in a sentence (cf. section 2.1.2), may have forms that are identical to those of **compound participles,** viz.

(1) The Present Passive Participle (formed by **being + a past participle)**
e.g. **being machined,**

(2) The Perfect Participle Active (formed by **having + a past participle)**
e.g. **having machined,**

(3) The Perfect Participle Passive (formed by **having been + a past participle)**
e.g. **having been machined.**

It can be seen from the foregoing discussion about the **'ing' form** that there is good reason to adhere to what has proved to be worthwhile: **the distinction between the g e r u n d and the p r e s e n t  p a r t i c i p l e.** If this well-established principle is disregarded or discarded, scientific ground is lost to wild speculations - rather than giving straightforward and clear definitions - as may be exemplified by the following attempt to define the item of **gerund**: "Gerunds are verb forms that end in -ing, -d, -ed, -n, -en, or -t and that function as nouns" (Picket/Laster 1984, 652). This definition is untenable, since the given grammatical morphemes, except '-ing', of course, reveal that the alleged gerund forms are in fact past participles. Furthermore, gerunds do not only function as **nouns** but also, for example, as **adverbials**, i.e. elements of clause structures (cf. Crystal 1980, 17). The implications of careless or imprecise definitions for the learning process need not be illustrated further.

### 1.5 The Aim of this Book

This book is intended for students of Science and Technology who have already acquired a good knowledge of general English and who wish to learn how to handle a variety of complex syntactic structures so as to identify, interpret, and use them in a subject-specific context of **SE**. The most obvious and the most widely recognized of these syntactic structures in ESL are the non-finite clauses, comprising gerundial constructions, participial constructions, and infinitival constructions, as well as verbless clauses and adjectival clauses. Since research into these structures is felt to be a matter of linguistic concern in the field of ESP, this book is also seen as a contribution towards establishing a '**SE** grammar'. Moreover, those engaged in the business of teaching ESP or translating or writing scientific papers, it is hoped, can make good use of it in their work.

Although this book has been designed to meet the requirements of students of ESP whose native language is German, it can equally well be used by any other English speaking learners who seek elucidation concerning the structures and uses of the syntactic items under discussion.

The guiding principle is to show each syntactic item and pertinent elements in bold type in order to mark their positions in the structures of authentic sentences. The examples used to illustrate the nature of the various syntactic items to be discussed have been drawn from a corpus of about one thousand five hundred sentences and sample texts, most of which were ascertained in a syntactic analysis of a large number of articles chosen at random in two large encyclopedias. They are provided with bibliographical details about the book title, volume, headword(s) or heading and page number of the entry in round brackets to set them apart from a small number of grammatical patterns and, more importantly, to facilitate the process of interpretation, once the special field referred to by the headword(s) or heading is known.

The two encyclopedias used for the analysis are:

VAN NOSTRAND´S SCIENTIFIC ENCYCLOPEDIA (1989), which covers the broad field of science in the expanse of approximately three thousand printed pages in two volumes, based on inputs from several hundred scientists, engineers, and educators, located worldwide, and HOW THINGS WORK - THE UNIVERSAL ENCYCLOPEDIA OF MACHINES (1980), which covers all the major sources of modern technology in the expanse of more than one thousand one hundred pages in two volumes. In the Foreword of volume 1 the reader learns that "the translation and adaptation of this book from the original German into English was conceived and carried out as a joint Anglo-American project, every effort being made to make the book useful to both American and British readers." It should be noted that the English version of the original German book 'Wie funktioniert das?' is much more comprehensive, which gives rise to the assumption that a considerable amount of the additional inputs must be due to some cooperation with British and American specialists.

This is not the place, however, to indulge in speculations on the number of contributors, merely because the reader does not learn anything about the number of experts involved in the joint project. From an ESP-point of view it is much more appropriate to emphasize the authenticity both in content and form of an important book that is valued by THE RIGHT HON. THE LORD RITCHIE-CALDER, Kalinga Prize winner for promoting the common understanding of science, in the Foreword of volume 2 as follows: "**How Things Work** is a valuable piece of communication (to use an overworked word) and, speaking professionally, a useful crib for science writers and for scientists and technologists as well."

There are two reasons for the choice of the text type 'encyclopedia'. In the first place, it is made up of a large number of articles which are grammatically independent texts written by independent specialists. With respect to text organization and register the articles are identical or very similar to those of individual articles, essays, papers, i.e. scholarly essays or lectures, etc. (cf. Sager et al. 1980, 159; Gläser 1990, 93) published in scientific and engineering journals and magazines, so that they can just as well be used as adequate and convenient sources for the study of syntactic features that are common to ESL.

In the second place, the text type of encyclopedia, which is usually easily available and therefore widely used as probably the most important type of reference books next to dictionaries, is produced to give special information to various readerships who, nevertheless, share the same interests, fields of activity, or occupation, students and experts in some branch of knowledge, for instance. Again, this text type, due to the nature of information conveyed, shares with other types of scientific literature typical *expository* features of ESL registers, such as *definition, interpretation, specification, classification, subdivision, cross-reference, cause and effect,* which can also be exploited for the learning process as soon as the analysis of syntactic structures makes them transparent.

The organization of this book aims at giving a detailed description of all linguistic data that are potentially relevant to a full understanding of the structural and functional role of special syntactic devices in ESL and attempts to raise the learners' consciousness about the processes involved in using a variety of syntactic options. By this I mean to sensitize the learners to the special use of language in which grammar is related to processes of thought, and to the role of particular grammatical properties in different language systems, thus helping them to respond positively to their bilingual situation and to recognize cross-linguistic differences more easily.

It should be called to mind that by parsing the structure of sentences we learn more about the peculiarities of English grammar in the field of **SE**. This is why each syntactic item, after being discussed or analysed and contextualized in English and German, is followed by a number of sample sentences to enable the reader to practise and improve the skill of parsing. The mental processes involved will pave the way for making use of syntactic structures, which are characteristic of and common in scientific and technical communication.

## 2. CLAUSE-REDUCING DEVICES

In science and technology isolated facts or events are seldom dealt with so that the 'simple sentence' as an appropriate syntactic unit for the formulation and dissemination of this kind of message is not often used. As a rule, the scientist or engineer is faced with a whole series of connected events, and he has to show **what the connection is**. He may have to show not only **what happens**, but also **how it happens, when it happens, why it happens**, and **what the effect of it is**. The result is that we usually find very long and complicated sentences of the 'complex sentence' type, i.e. "a sentence which contains one or more dependent clauses, in addition to its independent, or main clause" (Richards et al. 1985, 52). Complex sentences, therefore, are the appropriate syntactic units that enable a writer to formulate a coherent analysis, argument, description, etc. on the matter at issue.

Mention has already been made that one of the features of ESL is 'conciseness of style', which is mainly due to the prevalent use of clause-reducing devices, viz. **gerunds, participles**, and **infinitives** as well as certain **adjectival constructions**. In other words, dependent clauses such as 'relative clauses', 'adverbial clauses', and 'object clauses' in complex sentences are often dispensed with in favour of reduced or verbless clauses, which, however, are less transparent than the former and therefore occasionally difficult for the non-native learner of ESP to grasp.

With respect to the feature of 'economy' in the structure of sentences Sager/Dungworth (1980, 1078) point out that "the depersonalised nature of technical statements and their preoccupation with general truths independent of temporal factors greatly reduces the need for tenses, other than the present, and verbal constructions in general, thus making non-finite verb forms available for use in nominal and adjectival functions."

### 2.1 Gerundial Constructions

The gerund may be regarded as a hybrid because it has most characteristics of a noun, see section 2.1.1, but also some characteristics of a verb, see section 2.1.2. It shares the many-sided usability of the former and the lively expressiveness of the latter.

Knowledge of this double function is fundamental to its identification and interpretation since it provides the clues to answering the question why the gerund may be occasionally translated into German as a **noun, verbal noun, infinitive,** or, most certainly in connection with prepositions preceding it, as an **adverbial clause** or **adverb phrase.** Contextual clues as well as stylistic considerations ultimately decide the question of which of these possibilities to choose.

### 2.1.1 Nominal Characteristics of the Gerund

The **gerund** can be:

**(1)** the **subject** of a sentence or clause;

**(2)** the **complement** of a sentence;

**(3)** the **object** of a sentence or clause;

**(4)** preceded by the **definite article** and followed by the preposition **'of'** plus **object;**

**(5)** preceded by the **indefinite article;**

**(6)** qualified by a **demonstrative, possessive** or **indefinite pronoun;**

**(7)** qualified by an **adjective** preceding it;

**(8)** a pure **noun** and as such can form the **plural.**

**(1)** The gerund as **subject:**

(1.1) **Employing** fixed-pitch propellers in high-performance airplane design presents numerous problems. (NSE/I/PROPELLERS/63)
Der **Einsatz** von Festpropellern ist bei der Konstruktion von Hochleistungsflugzeugen mit zahlreichen Problemen verbunden.

(1.2) Small compressors may be operated with high compression ratios (8-12) if desired because cooling is more effective in small cylinders and mechanical strength is readily provided. (NSE/I/RECIPROCATING COMPRESSORS/60)

(1.3) Conveying the water from the penstock and directing the proper amount of it correctly against the runner requires first, a scroll case; second, a speed ring; and third, turbine gates. (NSE/I/ HYDRAULIC TURBINES/1486)

**(2)** The gerund as **complement:**

(2.1) The consequent effect of dissolved oxygen in feedwater is **pitting** of the internal surfaces. (NSE/I/FEEDWATER/OXYGEN CONTROL/1120)
Die Folge des gelösten Sauerstoffs im Speisewasser ist **Punktkorrosion** der Innenflächen.

(2.2) A simple and common method is known as resistance coupling. This is coupling in which resistors are used as the input and output impedances of the circuits being coupled. (NSE/I/AMPLIFIER/139)

(2.3) The most important bonding force in the crystalline phases in most ceramics is ionic bonding, the metallic atoms losing an outer electron to become positive ions; ... (NSE/I/CONVENTIONAL CERAMICS/ STRUCTURALS/556)

**(3)** The gerund as **object:**

(3.1) The difference in specific gravity of the solutions prevents, or at least retards, **mixing.** (NSE/I/GALVANIC CELL/1283)
Der Unterschied des spezifischen Gewichts verhindert oder zumindest verzögert **das Mischen.**

(3.2) Multi-stage compression may have cooling between the stages so the overall compression may be more isothermal than adiabetic.
(NSE/I/ CENTRIFUGAL COMPRESSORS/60)

(3.3 ) Ventilating fans usually are centrifugal because the application often requires overcoming considerable static pressure. (NSE/I/ FAN/1113)

There are verbs which only take the gerund after them, and there are relatively few verbs which allow both the gerund and the infinitive, depending on the meaning to be conveyed. The choice of the form of the object, i.e. either gerund or infinitive, is made "according to the same principles of *aspect* selection which apply to the choice of the progressive or simple form. Here the **-ing form** focuses on the on-going nature of a situation while the simple form/infinitive refers to the external aspect of a situation, namely its totality as an act, event or state" (Gramley 1988, 77).

It is interesting to note that among the verbs ascertained with the gerund there are several classes of semantically similar verbs such as verbs of *aspect* "which belong together by virtue of their reference to some aspect of an act, activity, event, process, etc., namely to its initial, middle or final phase" (ibid. 74), for example:

**start, begin, continue, finish, stop + gerund or infinitive; delay, postpone + gerund.**

Other classes are:

verbs of *causation*, e.g. **cause, permit, facilitate + gerund**; verbs of *inclusion*, e.g. **include, involve + gerund**; verbs of *non-accomplishment*, e.g. **avoid, prevent, eliminate, retard + gerund**.

Traditionally verbs are classified according to whether they take the gerund after them or allow the choice of both the gerund and the infinitive (e.g. Eckersley 1960; Lamprecht 1970). From a **SE** point of view important verbs of the former group are: **provide, require, practise, ensure, resist, risk, escape, correct, suggest, imagine, recall, mind, make,** and **have** (used as a full verb with the meaning of *possess*); relevant verbs of the latter group include: **need, intend, forget, neglect, regret, propose, stop, try, and remember.**

Lamprecht (1970, 280 - 281) points out that the verbs **stop, try,** and **remember** have different meanings, depending on whether they are used as gerunds or infinitives:

| | |
|---|---|
| **stop doing** | = *aufhören mit, beenden;* |
| **stop to do** | = *innehalten; etw. abbrechen, um etw. anderes zu tun;* |
| **try doing** | = *es mit etw. versuchen; ausprobieren; etw. versuchsweise tun;* |
| **try to do** | = *versuchen, etw. zu tun* |
| **remember doing** | = *sich erinnern, etw. getan zu haben* |
| **remember to do** | = *daran denken, nicht vergessen, etw. zu tun* |

Although the gerund as the object of a verb is purely substantival, it does not necessarily require a nominal translation into German, an infinitive may be preferred instead, as illustrated by the following examples.

(3.4) Some kinds of cells require **renewing** of the plates.

(a) Einige Arten von Elementen erfordern eine **Erneuerung** der Elektroden.

(b) Einige Arten von Elementen machen es erforderlich, die Elektroden **zu erneuern.**

(3.5) Others need only **recharging.**

(a) Andere erfordern nur eine **Nachladung.**

(b) Andere brauchen nur **wiederaufgeladen zu werden.**

**(4)** The gerund preceded by the **definite article** and followed by the preposition **'of'** plus **noun:**

(4.1) **The burning of this additional fuel** greatly increases the gas temperature and correspondingly the jet velocity, resulting in as much as 50% increase in thrust. (NSE/I/AIRPLANE/AUGMENTATION/65)

Die **Verbrennung dieses zusätzlichen Treibstoffs** erhöht stark die Gastemperatur und dementsprechend die Geschwindigkeit des Strahlflugzeugs, was zu einem Anstieg der Schubkraft um 50% führt.

(4.2 ) Brazing may be defined as the joining of metals through the use of heat and a filler metal whose melting temperature is above 840°F (45O°C), but below the melting point of the metals being joined. (NSE/I/BRAZING/428)

(4.3 ) In addition to assuring the convenience, comfort, and safety of non-flooded surfaces, adequate drainage is required ... to prevent the weakening of underlying foundations and ultimate collapse of all or parts of the structure.
(NSE/I/DRAINAGE SYSTEMS/934)

**(5)** The gerund preceded by the **indefinite article:**

This usage seems to be extremely rare as compared with the pattern at (4). Two examples can be given to furnish proof of it.

(5.1 ) ... the rest of the carbon dioxide (about 30%) is cooled to solid carbon dioxide snow (-79°C). This "snow" is sprayed on to the fire by the carbon dioxide gas and causes **a lowering of the temperature** to below the ignition point...
(HTW/I/FIRE EXTINGUISBERS/10)

... der Rest des Kohlendioxids (etwa 30%) erkaltet zu festem Kohlendioxidschnee (-79°C). Dieser "Schnee" wird durch das Kohlendioxidgas in das Feuer gesprüht und verursacht eine **Senkung der Temperatur** unterhalb des Zündpunkts.

(5.2) If a negative pressure gradient exists beyond the separation point, as it often does, there will be a reverse flow toward the separation point, all of which will produce a breaking away of the streamlines from the surface, leaving the surface between the two separation points, on either side of the body, in contact with air of random vortices and low pressure. (NSE/I/LAMINAR AND TURBULENT FLOW/46)

**(6)** The gerund qualified by a **demonstrative, possessive** or **indefinite pronoun:**

(6.1) **This preheating** of the gas and air enables the combustion temperature of the flame to be considerably raised. (HTW/I/STEEL/334)

**Das Vorerwärmen** des Gases und der Luft ermöglicht es, daß die Verbrennungstemperatur der Flamme beträchtlich erhöht werden kann.

(6.2) This descaling can be done by various mechanical methods (e.g., shot-blasting) or by pickling, i.e., immersion of the wire rod in a bath of dilute sulphuric or hydrochloric acid.

(HTW/I/WIRE MANUFACTURE/342)

(6.3) Forecasts usually are based upon assumptions that are subject to periodic change and **their reporting** is best left to the periodicals and thus are not detailed here.

(NSE/II/SOLAR ENERGY/ PHOTOVOLTAIC CONVERSION (SOLAR CELLS) /THIN FILMS/2636)

Voraussagen beruhen gewöhnlich auf Annahmen, die von periodischen Veränderungen abhängig sind, und **Berichte darüber** werden am besten den Zeitschriften überlassen und werden folglich hier nicht ausführlich erörtert.

(6.4) ...if a material is subjected to an alternating stress (such as a spring which is repeatedly and rapidly being compressed and released, and then compressed again), slip occurs in the actual particles of the material itself, which results in its having a very much lower elastic limit. (OJE/VIII/ENGINEERING DESIGN/138)

(6.5) The directional gyroscope ensures directional stability of the compass system; the flux valve senses the earth's magnetic field and transmits signals which correct **any wandering** of the gyroscope. (HTW/I/AIR NAVIGATION/568)

Der Kurskreisel gewährleistet die Richtungsstabilität der Kompaßanlage. Die Induktionssonde tastet das Magnetfeld der Erde ab und überträgt Signale, die **ein Wandern** des Kreisels korrigieren.

(6.6) In most systems all load and unload as well as refixturing operations must be done at special stations and not on the machine tools themselves. Thus, each fixturing requires the part leaving a machine, traveling to a special station, and then traveling back to continue being machined. (NSE/II/DESIGNING FOR NC PRODUCTION/2037)

**(7)** The gerund qualified by an **adjective**:

(7.1) **Careful streamlining** and reduction of parts exposed to the air stream are ways of reducing parasite drag. (NSE/I/AERODYNAMICS AND AEROSTATICS/DRAG/48)

**Sorgfältige strömungsgünstige Gestaltung** und Reduzierung von Bauteilen, die dem Fahrtwind ausgesetzt sind, sind Methoden zur Verringerung des schädlichen Widerstands.

(7.2) Continuous processing produces sheets of more uniform thickness and essentially eliminates warping. (NSE/I/CASTING OF PLASTICS/521)

(7.3) Eccentric mounting causes a frequency-modulated signal to be superimposed on top of the encoder output signal.
(NSE/I/ENCODER/OTHER ENCODER PROBLEM AREAS/1065)

**(8)** The gerund as a pure **noun**:

A number of gerund forms have become pure nouns and as such can form the plural, e.g.:

| | |
|---|---|
| coating(s) | *Überzug* |
| protective coating | *Schutzüberzug* |
| casting(s) | *Gußteil, Gußstück* |
| casing(s) (Eng.) | *Gehäuse* |
| turnings | *Drehspäne* |
| filings | *Feilspäne* |

(8.1) Important to efficiency of absorption and pressure drop is the type of packing used. (NSE/I/ABSORPTION(PROCESS)/7)

(8.2) A rotating impeller mounted in a casing and revolved at high speed... (NSE/I/CENTRIFUGAL COMPRESSORS/60)

### 2.1.2 Verbal Characteristics of the Gerund

The gerund

**(1)** can take a **direct object;**

**(2)** can be modified by an **adverb;**

**(3)** can be in the **passive;**

**(4)** can be in the **perfect.**

**(1)** The gerund followed by a **direct object:**

On the sentence level this structure constitutes a close syntactic unit in that the gerund, strictly speaking, is the grammatical object of a sentence or clause because of its position after a **predicative verb** (refer back to (3) in section 2.1.1.) or a **preposition** (see section 2.1.3), while the following **direct object** functions as its complement.

(1.1) The rough translation of a sentence involves **comparing the words** read from a punched tape with the entries in the "dictionary". (HTW/I/TRANSLATION PROGRAMME FOR A PROGRAMME-CONTROLLED COMPUTER/286)

Die Grobübersetzung eines Satzes umfaßt **das Vergleichen der Wörter,** die von einem Lochstreifen abgelesen werden, mit den Eintragungen im "Wörterbuch".

(1.2) Ventilating fans usually are centrifugal because the application often requires overcoming considerable static pressure. (NSE/I/FAN/1113)

(1.3) Major international conferences began having a crucial influence on operator algebra theory in the mid-1960s. (NSE/II/MATHEMATICS/1808)

**(2)** The gerund modified by an **adverb:**

(2.1) Prior to **briefly describing** current battery research, it is in order here to review the lead-acid battery situation further... (NSE/I/BATTERY REQUIREMENTS/1005)

Vor **einer kurzen Beschreibung** des gegenwertigen Standes der Batterieforschung erscheint es hier angebracht, den gegenwärtigen Entwicklungsstand der Bleibatterie zu besprechen...

(2.2) The hydrogen can be obtained by countercurrently scrubbing the gas mixture in a packed or tray column with monoethanolamine which absorbs the carbon dioxide. (NSE/I/ABSORPTION(PROCESS)/7)

(2.3) The situation is more complex for a continuous information source because the differential entropy is only a relative measure of information rather than an absolute one. Thus, simply multiplying the bits per sample ... by the number of samples per second, does not yield a number that can be interpreted properly as information rate. (NSE/I/INFORMATION THEORY/1544)

**(3)** The gerund in the **passive:**

(3.1) Soldering is the process of joining metal parts by means of a molten filler metal (solder) whose melting point is lower than that of the metals to be joined. The latter are wetted by the molten filler without themselves **being melted** (as in welding). (HTW/II/SOLDERING/138)

Löten ist ein Verfahren zum Vereinigen von metallischen Teilen mit Hilfe eines geschmolzenen Zusatzmetalls (Lot), dessen Schmelztemperatur niedriger ist als diejenige der zu vereinigenden Metalle. Die letzteren werden von dem geschmolzenen Lot benetzt, ohne selbst **geschmolzen zu werden** (wie beim Schweißen).

(3.2) Also, the spring must prevent the wheels being lifted off the road as a sudden jolt occurs and thus safeguard the "grip" or "ground adhesion" of the vehicle. (HTW/I/SPRINGING, AXLES, WHEEL SUSPENSION/502)

(3.3) One of the earliest sensitive electroscopes consists of two narrow strips of gold-leaf hanging together in a glass jar. Upon being charged, they stand apart on account of their mutual repulsion. (NSE/I/ELECTROSCOPE/1049)

**(4)** The gerund in the **perfect:**

(4.1) Alpha rays consist of alpha particles, which are the nuclei of helium atoms which are positively charged on account of **having lost** two electrons. (HTW/I/RADIOACTIVITY/456)
Alphastrahlung besteht aus Alphateilchen, welche die Kerne von Heliumatomen sind und welche positiv geladen sind, weil **sie** zwei Elektronen **verloren haben.**

(4.2) In ramjet engines, combustion is continuous after having been started by spark ignition or other methods. (NSE/I/AIRPLANE/RAMJET ENGINES/67)

Compared with the verbal characteristics given at (1) and (2) the passive and perfect forms of the gerund are of relatively rare occurrence, unless they are preceded by a preposition.

### 2.1.3 The Gerund as the Object of a Preposition

The only part of a verb that can be the object of a preposition is the gerund. The prepositions used with the gerund vary largely both in form and meaning. The gerund is most frequently preceded by **simple prepositions** which consist of one word, such as **by, with, without, on, upon, after, before, in, during, at, for,** and **besides.** But the gerund can also be prededed by **complex prepositions** which "may be subdivided into two- and three-word sequences. In two-word sequences, the first word (which usually is relatively stressed) is an adverb, adjective, or conjunction, and the second word a simple preposition" (Quirk et al. 1985, 669). With three-word sequences the authors (ibid. 670) also include complex prepositions where the noun is preceded by a definite or indefinite article. The examples dealt with in this chapter include **due to, on account of, in the event of, apart from, in addition to, instead of, with regard to,** and **prior to.**

The order in which the structure **preposition + gerund** will be itemized has been chosen according to both interlingual and intralingual considerations. The former bring differences between English and German structures into focus in that

**(1) preposition + gerund in En** correlates functionally and semantically with **syntactic units in Ge** which include **adverb phrases, adverbial clauses, and infinitive clauses,**

whereas the latter refer to semantic relationships and/or the relative frequency of occurrence of individual prepositions + gerund as well as to a noticeable number of structures which consist of

**(2) noun + preposition + gerund,**

**(3) verb + preposition + gerund,** and

**(4) adjective + preposition + gerund.**

What matters in (1), see below, is to bear in mind that an adverbial clause in En (a) can be shortened by the structure **preposition + gerund** (b) which in Ge can be represented either by an adverb phrase with a verbal noun (c) or by an adverbial clause (d), e.g.

(a) Before the engine is started ...

(b) **Before starting the engine...**

(c) Vor Anlassen des Motors ...

(d) Bevor der Motor angelassen wird ...

Note that the structure **preposition + gerund** retains the *passive* meaning that is overt in (a) and needs to be considered if (d) is chosen as translation into Ge. In place of the passive construction the Ge indefinite pronoun **man,** which only occurs in the nominative case and thus can function as the subject of a clause, may be preferred:

(e) Bevor **man** den Motor anläßt...

**(1) Preposition + gerund in En allowing correspondences with adverb phrases, adverbial clauses or infinitive clauses in Ge**

Compare:

(1.1) **'By' + gerund** is used to express *means, method* or *instrument.* Ge alternative structures are either an adverbial clause of manner introduced by **'indem', 'dadurch, daß'** or an adverb phrase consisting of **'durch'** + verbal noun.

(1.1.1) In another technique the sheet metal is shaped **by being distended in a mold under radial internal pressure.** (RTW/II/SHEET-METAL WORK/142)
In einem anderen Verfahren wird die Blechtafel **dadurch** geformt, **daß sie** unter radialem Innendruck in einer Form **aufgebläht wird.**

(1.1.2) Ductile metals hardened by cold-working may be softened by annealing. (NSE/I/ANNEALING/167)

(1.1.3) Programming is accomplished by manually initiating signals to the servo valves to move the various axes into a desired position and then recording the output of the feedback devices into the memory of the controller.
(NSE/II/ROBOT CONTROL SYSTEMS/2455)

(1.2) **'With' + gerund** is used to indicate *means* or *method.* It apparently occurs less frequently than **'without' + gerund**, which expresses the equivalent negative meaning. The structures in Ge vary greatly, depending on which of the two prepositions is used. Thus **'with' + gerund** corresponds to an adverb phrase such as **'mit'** or **'für'** + verbal noun, whereas **'without' + gerund** usually requires a clause in Ge. This can be either an infinitive clause introduced by **'ohne zu'** or an adverbial clause of manner introduced by **'ohne daß'.**

(1.2.1) There are problems **with sealing** at the point where the piston rods leave the closed system containing the working fluid;...
(NSE/I/INTERNAL COMBUSTION ENGINE/1581)
Es gibt Probleme **mit dem Abdichten** an dem Punkt, wo die Kolbenstangen das abgeschlossene System verlassen, das das Arbeitsmedium enthält.

(1.2.2) The implanted atoms are apparently transported into the metal as a tool wears. Thus, the technology is of large interest in connection with improving cutting tools and bearings.

(1.2.3) The maximum stress that can be applied **without causing permanent deformation** upon release of the load is the elastic limit. (NSE/II/TENSION TEST/2801)
Die maximale Beanspruchung, die ausgeübt werden kann, **ohne bleibende Verformung** nach dem Aufhören der Krafteinwirkung **zu verursachen,** ist die Elastizitätsgrenze.

(1.2.4) The ability to reprogram means that the mistakes made in the program can be corrected without having to discard parts. (NSE/II/MEMORY (ELECTRONIC)EPROM/1819)

(1.2.5) This emission from electrons from an incandescent metal ... can most suitably be made to take place in a vacuum. This prevents oxidation of the very hot surface of the metal and allows the electrons to emerge unobstructed, i.e., without colliding with, or being neutralised by, gas molecules and ions of air.
(HTW/I/THERMIONIC (VACUUM) TUBE/70)

(1.3) **'On', 'upon',** or **'after' + gerund** are used to denote *after* and *time after.* The Ge structures include an adverbial clause of time introduced by **'nachdem'** and an adverb phrase consisting of **'nach'** + (verbal) noun.

(1.3.1) **On bombarding certain surfaces by electrons** it may happen that each impinging electron expels several electrons from the struck surface.
(NSE/I/ELECTRON MULTIPLICATION/1044)
**Nach dem Bombardieren bestimmter Oberflächen durch Elektronen** kann es passieren, daß jedes auftreffende Elektron mehrere Elektronen von der getroffenen Oberfläche abstößt.

(1.3.2) On passing from the liquid to the vaporous state, every liquid absorbs heat and subsequently gives off this heat again on condensing.
(HTW/I/ REFRIGERATORS/256)

(1.3.3) Upon coming in contact with the phosphor, small amounts of hydrogen combine with the oxygen in the air to excite bright luminescence in the phosphor.
(NSE/I/HYDROGEN AS A HEATING FUEL/1495)

(1.3.4) **After being cooled to 393°C in the heat exchangers,** the primary sodium is pumped back into the reactor where it again repeats the circuit
(NSE/II/NUCLEAR POWER/LMFBR DESIGN PRINCIPLE/2018)
**Nachdem das Primärnatrium in den Wärmetauschern auf 393°C abgekühlt worden ist,** wird es in den Reaktor zurückgepumpt, wo es den Kreislauf erneut durchläuft.

(1.3.5) After undergoing refraction, parallel rays appear to come from one point (F), while rays emerging from a point will, after passing through the lens, appear to emerge from another point. ... Conversely, rays which pass through (or emerge from) become parallel after being refracted by the lens. (HTW/I/LENSES/132)

(1.4) **'Before' + gerund** and **'after' + gerund** (look back to (1.3)) indicate *relations between two times* or *events* and thus have opposite meanings. Ge alternative structures to match **'before' + gerund** are either a clause of time introduced by **'bevor'** or an adverb phrase consisting of **'vor'** + (verbal) noun.

(1.4.1) The creep motion of the car **before stopping at a floor** is obtained by changing over to a lower speed of the motor. (HTW/I/ LIFT (ELEVATOR)/218)
Die Kriechgeschwindigkeit des Fahrstuhls **vor dem Anhalten in einem Geschoß** wird durch das Umschalten in eine niedrigere Motordrehzahl bewirkt.

(1.4.2) This hot air recirculates continuously, i.e., it is drawn into the compressor again after leaving the turbine. However, the air must be cooled before entering the compressor, otherwise the blading of the latter would soon be destroyed as a result of operating at excessively high temperatures. (HTW/I/GAS TURBINES/42)

(1.4.3) This mixture of gas and air is burned over the hearth; the hot waste gases flow through flues on the other side of the furnace and are discharged up the chimney. Before being discharged, however, the gases give off a considerable proportion of their heat to - initially cold - brick-lined heating chambers. (HTW/I/STEEL/ 334)

(1.5) **'In' + gerund** is used to denote *same time*. The potential structures in Ge comprise an adverbial clause of time introduced by **'wenn'**, a clause of manner introduced by **'indem'** and an adverb phrase consisting of **'bei'** + verbal noun. **'In' + gerund** can also be used to indicate a *purpose* (see (1.7) below) or *cause-effect relationship* which Sager/Dungworth (1980, 1087) exemplify by:

This model differs in being more efficient.

Dieses Modell unterscheidet sich durch größere Effizienz.

(1.5.1) Annealing is often an important intermediate step **in producing metals by cold deformation.** (NSE/I/ANNEALING/167)
Glühen ist häufig eine wichtige Zwischenphase **bei der Erzeugung metallischer Werkstoffe durch Kaltumformen**.

(1.5.2) In falling through the atmosphere, rain water (meteoric water) picks up small amounts of oxygen, carbon dioxide, and other gases (notably in areas where air pollutants are present). (NSE/I/EROSION(GEOLOGY)/CHEMICAL EROSION/1087)

(1.5.3) The other and most commonly used concept in determining propeller performance is the blade element theory. ... The efficiency of a propeller in converting engine power to thrust is obviously of tremendous importance in airplane performance. (NSE/I/AIRPLANE/63)

(1.6) **'During' + gerund** is used to suggest *duration*, while **'at' + gerund** narrows *duration* down to up to *a point of time*. This structure usually corresponds to an adverb phrase in Ge which consists of **'bei'** or **'während'** + verbal noun, whereas an adverbial clause of time introduced by the formally identical conjunction **'während'** seems to be out of place.

(1.6.1) Stresses that develop **during the casting** can be controlled by very slowly cooling the casting over a period of 24 hours or longer. (NSE/I/CASTING OF PLASTICS/521)
Spannungen, die **während des Gießens** entstehen, können durch sehr langsames Abkühlen des Gußstücks in einem Zeitraum von 24 Stunden oder länger kontrolliert werden.

(1.6.2) A high yield-strength ratio, resulting from cold drawing, minimizes plastic flow during machining, thus permitting better utilization of machine tool energy. (NSE/I/COLD WORKING AND HEAT TREATING STEELS/ 1616)

(1.6.3) A further advantage is that the electric motor develops its highest torque (turning moment applied to the wheels) at starting. (HTW/I/ ELECTRIC LOCOMOTIVE/526)

(1.6.4) For a given path length, process analyzers which use the microphone detectors are more effective than those analyzers which use solid state detectors and optical filters at measuring low concentrations of gases which have a lot of structure in their absorption band. (NSE/I/MICROPHONE DETECTORS/1552)

(1.7) **'For' + gerund** is used to indicate *purpose.* There is a corresponding paraphrase with the infinitive clause **'(in order) to'**, which is identical with the Ge structure **'um zu'** + infinitive. **'For' + gerund** correlates with a Ge adverb phrase consisting of **'für'** or **'zur'** + verbal noun, but it allows the translation as infinitive clause as well.

(1.7.1) Basically, the alternator is a device **for converting mechanical into electrical energy.** (NSE/I/ALTERNATOR/107)
Im Grunde ist der Generator eine Maschine **zur Umwandlung von mechanischer Energie in elektrische Energie**.

(1.7.2) In terms of metals, the art of casting is one of the oldest methods for making metal parts and is still used extensively even though numerous other methods for producing shaped metal products, such as forging, rolling, and extruding, have been developed. (NSE/I/CASTING/520)

(1.7.3) A different type of device is the indirect-acting thermostat, which uses an auxiliary source of power (e.g. electricity or compressed air) for transmitting the impulses for effecting the change in temperature. (HTW/I/THERMOSTAT/16)

(1.8) **'Besides' + gerund** is used to denote *addition.* This structure is matched in Ge by an adverb phrase consisting of **'außer'** or **'abgesehen von'** + (verbal) noun or the phrase **'abgesehen davon'** + object clause introduced by the conjunction **'daß'**.

(1.8.1) **Besides taking up far less space** transistorised systems have the advantage of dispensing with the filament current. (HTW/I/ SEMICONDUCTORS/78)
**Außer der Inanspruchnahme von bedeutend weniger Raum** bieten transistorisierte Systeme den Vorteil des Verzichts auf Heizstrom.

(1.8.2) Besides wearing the self-contained space suit, the astronaut is additionally enclosed within a fully air-conditioned and temperature-controlled capsule.
(HTW/II/SPACE SUITS AND SPACE CAPSULES/ 372)

(1.8.3) Where accurate alignment is not possible, a flexible coupling is used; it allows for a certain amount of misalignment, besides acting as a shock absorber for vibrations and jerks in torque transmission. (HTW/II/COUPLINGS/188)

A survey of the ascertained complex prepositions used with the gerund in the examples given below shows their meanings and the equivalent expressions in Ge as follows:

| **Preposition(s)** | **Meaning(s)** | = **Equivalent Ge Expression(s)** |
|---|---|---|
| **due to, on account of** | *cause, reason, effect* | **aufgrund, wegen** |
| **in the event of** | *condition* | **im Falle** |
| **apart from** | *exception* | **abgesehen von, bis auf, außer** |
| **in addition to** | *additon* | **außer, zusätzlich zu** |
| **instead of** | *abandonment* | **statt, anstelle von** |
| **with regard to** | *respect* | **in bezug auf** |
| **prior to** | *time before* | **vor, bevor** |

(1.9) **'due to'** or **'on account of' + gerund**

The blue colour of the sky is due to scattering of sunlight on its way through the atmosphere,...
(HTW/I/REFLECTION, REFRACTION AND DIFFRACTION OF LIGHT/130)

Alpha rays consist of alpha particles, which are the nuclei of helium atoms which are positively charged on account of having lost two electrons.
(HTW/I/RADIOACTIVITY/456)

(1.10) **'in the event of' + gerund**

In the event of overwinding, the cage is slowed down and braked by such means as thickening the cage-guide rods in the top part of the headframe.
(HTW/II/WINDING/70)

(1.11) **'apart from' + gerund**

A vertical milling machine may be of the knee type and, apart from having a vertical spindle, is generally similar to the horizontal milling machine.
(HTW/II/MILLING MACHINE/186)

(1.12) **'in addition to' + gerund**

If the coupling, in addition to presenting a curved characteristic, also develops a so-called damping action, its recovery characteristic ... will differ from that of the characteristic for initial deformation. (HTW/II/COUPLINGS/192)

(1.13) **'instead of' + gerund**

In some valves the stem, instead of being provided with a disc, ends in a conical point which is inserted into the hole of the seat and closes it when the stem is screwed out of the valve body. (HTW/I/VALVES, COCKS AND TAPS/230)

(1.14) **'with regard to' + gerund**

With regard to reducing the resistance, one is soon up against a limit, because for reasons of economy and weight it is of course not possible to increase the thickness of the conductors indefinitely.
(HTW/I/OVERHEAD TRANSMISSION LINES/84)

(1.15) **'prior to' + gerund**

The change-over from altitude readings to height readings is effected prior to landing.
(HTW/I/AIR NAVIGATION/568)

**(2) Noun + preposition + gerund**

In **SE** this construction is widely used with abstract nouns most frequently followed by **'of' + gerund** (a). In this case the potential structures in Ge are of two kinds: the structurally equivalent attribute with the noun in the genitive (b) and the infinitive clause (c). Compare:

(a) ... **the problem of transmitting this information** from one place to another.
(NSE/I/INFORMATION THEORY/1542)

(b) ... **das Problem der Übermittlung dieser Information** von einem Ort zum anderen.

(c) ... **das Problem, diese Information** von einem Ort zum anderen **zu übermitteln.**

The structure 'of transmitting this information' comprises grammatically preposition + gerund + direct object which form a close syntactic unit functioning as attribute. This type of postmodification by means of an **'of phrase'** may sometimes have an alternative construction with the **'infinitive clause'.** For example, 'the ability of making joints' in the following sentence (d) may well be replaced by 'the ability to make joints'.

(d) Silver solders or brazing alloys have **the ability of making joints far stronger and more durable** than common soft solder (such as lead-tin) alloys.
(NSE/II/ USES OF SILVER/2587)
**Die Verwendung von Silberlot oder Hartlot gestattet es, viel festere und haltbarere Verbindungen herzustellen,** als es mit herkömmlichem Weichlot (z.B. Lötzinn) möglich wäre.

The following are abstract nouns whose meanings commonly involve *human judgement* which is logically linked with the generalizing function of 'preposition + gerund'.

(2.1) **This method of charging** is known as electrostatic induction.
(HTW/I/ELECTROSTATICS/52)

(2.2) **the process of dyeing** (NSE/I/ADSORPTION/43)

(2.3) **One way of defining the lower limit of long timber columns ...**
(NSE/I/COLUMN(STRUCTURAL)/705)

Note that **'way'** is frequently used in the plural:

(2.4) **ways of reducing parasite drag** (NSE/I/DRAG/48)

(2.5) the use of hydrogen as **a means or mode of storing and transporting energy**
(NSE/I/HYDROGEN AS AN ENERGY TRANSPORTER/1495)

(2.6) **the purpose of supporting moving loads** (NSE/I/BRIDGE/STRUCTURAL/437)

(2.7) **the primary objective of thickening** (NSE/I/CLASSIFYING/(PROCESS)/647)

(2.8) **the possibility of integrating and interlocking manufacturing operations** on a corporate and plantwide basis (NSE/I/CONTRIBUTION OF AUTOMATION TO ENGINEERING AND SCIENCE/291)

(2.9) each ground station must have the **capability of transmitting (and receiving with a mesh network)** at a data rate
(NSE/II/ SATELLITES/NETWORKING/2506)

(2.10) **the ability of ionizing radiation** (NSE/I/DOSIMETER/RADIATION/931)

(2.11) **the advantage of not using up time** moving the beam over areas
(NSE/I/ELECTRON BEAM LITHOGRAPHY/VECTOR SCAN METHOD/1038)

(2.12) **the advantage of being able to work on the rather low-grade, high-ash coal**
(NSE/I/COAL CONVERSION PROCESS/677)

(2.13) **the disadvantages of having a low operating pressure and taking up much space**
(HTW/I/STEAM BOILERS/36)

(2.14) **the difficulties of focusing a beam**
(NSE/I/FUSION POWER/BACKGROUND ON INERTIAL CONFINEMENT/1267)

(2.15) this may involve **a risk of jamming and locking of the brake** (HTW/I/BRAKES/514)

(2.16) the spacecraft traveling at high speed will be **in danger of being "bounced off" the earth's atmosphere** (HTW/II/REENTRY AND ABLATION/370)

(2.17) a flowing medium...produces a rotary motion as **a result of being deflected by rings of blading** mounted on a rotor... the blading ... would soon be destroyed as **a result of operating at excessively high temperatures** (HTW/I/GAS TURBINES/42)

(2.18) **On completion of filling,** the converter is swung to the upright position.
(HTW/I/STEEL/336)

(2.19) **the ease of processing and marketing foods** (NSE/I/ADDITIVES(FOOD)/36)

(2.20) **the additional attraction of decreasing air pollution/the option of using hydrogen**
(NSE/I/HYDROGEN AS ENERGY SOURCE FOR MOTIVE POWER/1494)

(2.21) **At the temperature of firing,** feldspar undergoes a gradual change from the crystalline to the glassy state, the rate depending upon **the time of heating** and the temperature..(NSE/I/CONVENTIONAL CERAMICS(STRUCTURALS)/555)

(2.22) **the angle of normal gliding** (NSE/I/HIGH-LIFT DEVICES/47)

(2.23) **this type of focusing of moving charged particles**
(NSE/I/ALTERNATING GRADIENT FOCUSING/106)

(2.24) **the function of damping the objectional spring oscillations**
(HTW/I/SHOCK ABSORBERS/508)

(2.25) **the era of practically achieving this goal**
(NSE/II/SOLAR ENERGY/PHOTOVOLTAIC CONVERSION/2636)

Examples with other prepositions than 'of' show the gerund construction as object:

(2.26) **There is no difficulty in visualising the transformation of pressure head into velocity head at the nozzle**, nor of understanding the push, or impulse, that is given to the buckets by the stream of water. (NSE/I/HYDRAULIC TURBINES/1458)

**Es ist nicht schwer, sich die Umwandlung** der statischen Druckhöhe in die dynamische Geschwindigkeitshöhe an der Düse **vorzustellen,** und auch nicht, **den Druck zu verstehen,** den das strömende Wasser auf die Schaufeln ausübt.

(2.27) **Experimental approaches to activating helium and trapping the helium molecules** in a hydrocarbon wax... (NSE/II/ROCKET PROPELLANTS/2466)

(2.28) Leading automotive manufacturers in recent years have directed **considerable research toward determining how the detailed shapes of various areas of a vehicle ... affect aerodynamic drag, with particular emphasis on improving fuel economy...** (NSE/I/DRAG STUDIES IN THE AUTOMOTIVE FIELD/49)

(2.29) quadrupole magnets ... have **no effect on deflecting the particles** ... (NSE/II/SYNCHROTRONS/2142)

(2.30) **the safety of a masonry dam against overturning** (NSE/I/ FACTOR OF SAFETY/1111)

**(3) Verb + preposition + gerund**

Basically this construction consists of a prepositional verb or, strictly speaking, a lexical verb followed by a preposition, with which it is semantically and/or syntactically associated, and the gerund as the object of the preposition (3.1). The sequence of the words involved is firmly established, even if a phrasal verb, i.e. a verbal construction consisting of a lexical verb plus an adverb particle, precedes the gerund (3.2).
Notice that a phrasal verb permits of shifting the particle from its position after the verb to the position after the object, if the latter is a noun phrase instead of a gerund. Compare:

**Turn on** the central heating. **Turn** the central heating **on. Turn it on**.

In **SE** ample use is made of prepositional verbs plus gerund as distinct from that of phrasal verbs plus gerund. This applies also to an extended type of prepositional verbs which has a noun phrase as the direct object of the verb followed by the preposition plus gerund (3.3).
Moreover, a special feature is the prepositional passive which, like any other pattern in the passive voice, is used in order to give the object of a transitive verb prominence by making it the subject of the passive verb phrase, leaving the preposition in its post-verbal position (3.4). However, the examples given to illustrate the importance of the prepositional passive in **SE** give rise to the assumption that many prepositional verbs are exclusively or preferably used in the passive voice, such as **'be subjected to'**, **'be based on'**, and **'be directed toward'**, whereas

structurally identically phrases show **'be'** linked with **predicative adjectives** such as **'be known as'**, **'be confined to'**, **'be devoted to'**, and **'be accustomed to'** (or, usually in general English, **'get/become accustomed to'**) whose verbal origin is evident, and that is why they are inluded in this section rather than allocating them to the adjectival structures at (4).

(3.1) **Prepositional verb + gerund**

This construction involves the following verbs:

| | |
|---|---|
| **consist of** | **bestehen aus** |
| **consist in** | **bestehen in** |
| **depend on** | **abängen von** |
| **persist in** | **anhalten, fortdauern** |
| **aim at** | **richten auf, zielen auf; vorhaben, etw. zu tun** |
| **refer to** | **beziehen auf** |
| **respond to** | **reagieren auf** |
| **attach to** | **beimessen, zuschreiben** |

Note that the Ge verbs suggest only basic potential meanings which need not necessarily match the contextual meanings of their En counterparts. This is also valid for the Ge verbs given at (3.3) and (3.4). Consider, for instance, the Ge translation of the last sentence in the following short passage:

> The liquids used in the chemical industries differ considerably in physical and chemical properties and it has been necessary to develop a wide variety of pumping equipment. We can consider these either as positive displacement or **centrifugal pumps**. In the former... . In this group... . **The centrifugal type depends on giving the liquid a high kinetic energy** which is then converted as efficiently as possible into pressure energy. (Coulson/Richardson 1956, 104)
>
> **Die Kreiselpumpe beruht auf dem Prinzip, der Flüssigkeit eine hohe kinetische Energie zu verleihen**, die dann so wirksam wie möglich in Druckenergie umgesetzt wird.

Notice, too, how in this text cohesion is provided by using a formally varied but semantically identical substitute as backward textual reference, viz. **"The centrifugal type"**, in order to avoid repeating the same wording when referring back or taking up the information given in a clause element of a preceding sentence, viz. **"centrifugal pumps"**.

(3.1.1) Essentially, the process **consists of passing the metal through (between) two rolls** which are revolving at the same peripheral speed, but in opposite direction. (NSE/I/ROLLING/1611).
Im Prinzip **besteht das Verfahren darin, daß das metallische Werkstück durch zwei Walzen geschoben wird**, die sich mit der gleichen Umfangsgeschwindigkeit drehen, aber in entgegengesetzter Richtung.

(3.1.2) Consideration of the requirements for equilibrium consists in balancing centrifugal forces against static pressures derived from Bernoulli´s theorem ...
(NSE/I/THEORY OF AERODYNAMIC CIRCULATION/51)

(3.1.3) Some plastic casting processes depend upon melting and solidifying, as with metals; ...
(NSE/I/CASTING OF PLASTICS/521)

(3.1.4) ... steel will retain a substantial proportion of the magnetism it acquires and thus form a permanent magnet, in which the magnetic domains persist in retaining their aligned orientation after the external magnetic field which produced this orientation has been removed. (HTW/II/ELECTROMAGNETS/502)

(3.1.5) Because of the restraint of the diaphragm at its edges, where it is gripped in its mounting, the fidelity of the reproduction is adversely affected, however. The further development of the loudspeaker therefore had to aim at achieving, as far as possible, unrestrained vibration of the diaphragm. (HTW/I/LOUDSPEAKER/82)

(3.1.6) REVEGETATION. Generally refers to the purposeful seeding and planting of an area that once was covered with grass, trees, shrubs, forbs, etc., but which was denuded of vegetation because of natural disturbance... (NSE/II/REVEGETATION/2434)

(3.1.7) A relay of this kind responds differently to energising currents flowing in different directions. (HTW/I/RELAY/90)

(3.1.8) Just how much lack of sharpness is acceptable will depend on how much the picture is to be enlarged and on how much importance the observer attaches to distinguishing minute details in the picture. (HTW/I/DEPTH OF FIELD(DEPTH OF FOCUS)/158)

(3.2) **Phrasal verb + gerund**

**The oscillations do not,** however, **go on increasing indefinitely**, but are limited by energy losses... (HTW/I/RESONANCE/ECHO/184)
**Die Schwingungen nehmen** jedoch **nicht unbegrenzt zu**, sondern werden durch Energieverluste begrenzt...

Note that the meaning of '**go on doing**' is '**etw. weitermachen, fortsetzen**' as opposed to the meaning of '**go on to do**', namely '**dazu übergehen, etw. (anderes) zu tun**'.

(3.3) **Verb + direct object + preposition + gerund**

The following verbs used in this construction are noteworthy:

| | |
|---|---|
| **prevent sth from doing sth** | **hindern an** |
| **protect sth from doing sth** | **schützen vor** |
| **keep sth from doing sth** | **abhalten von; hindern an** |

(3.3.1) **To prevent steam from also flowing back into the boiler,** steam traps are installed in this pipe. (HTW/I/STEAM HEATING/224)
**Um zu vermeiden, daß der Dampf in den Kessel zurückströmt,** sind Kondensationswasserableiter in diesem Leitungsrohr installiert.

(3.3.2) The gas flow controller keeps the rate of supply of gas to the burner constant and protects the appliance from overloading.
(HTW/I/GAS-FIRED WATER HEATER(GEYSER)/248)

(3.3.3) At elevated temperature, the solubility of water increases to 12-25%, depending upon the type of fat. At the higher temperatures, high pressures also are necessary to keep the water from flashing into steam.
(NSE/II/SOAPS/HYDROLYZER PROCESS/2610)

(3.4) **The prepositional passive + gerund**

| | |
|---|---|
| **be subjected to** | **einer Sache unterworfen sein** |
| **be based on** | **beruhen auf** |
| **be directed toward** | **gerichtet sein auf** |
| **be aimed at** | **gerichtet sein auf** |
| **be reduced to** | **beschränkt sein auf** |
| **be known as** | **bekannt sein als** |
| **be confined to** | **begrenzt sein auf** |
| **be devoted to** | **verwenden auf, bestimmen für** |
| **be accustomed to** | **etw. gewohnt sein** |

(3.4.1) When light, x-rays, or other electromagnetic radiation enters a body of matter, it experiences in general two types of attenuation. **Part of it is subjected to scattering,** being reflected in all directions, while another portion is absorbed by being converted into other forms of energy. (NSE/I/ABSORPTION COEFFICIENT/6)

Wenn Lichtstrahlen, Röntgenstrahlen oder andere elektromagnetische Strahlen auf einen Körper treffen, unterliegen sie im allgemeinen zwei Arten der materiellen Abschwächung. **Ein Teil von ihnen ist der Streuung unterworfen**, indem er in alle Richtungen reflektiert wird, während ein anderer Teil durch Umwandlung in andere Energieformen absorbiert wird.

(3.4.2) The satellites used in the Lunar Orbiter program relied on astronavigation, based on using the star Canopus (visible in the southern hemisphere) as a fixed point of reference...(HTW/II/INERTIAL NAVIGATION/374)

(3.4.3) Research is also directed toward improving powertrains. (NSE/I/BATTERY DEVELOPMENTS/1006)

(3.4.4) This technique too is aimed at reducing turbulence and thus producing a better-quality ingot. (HTW/II/CASTING/96)

(3.4.5) The outcome to a coalition can then be determined on the assumption that those outside the coalition will combine to oppose it. The problem is then reduced to studying which coalitions will form, and what payments should be made to each member of the coalition to prevent him from being attracted by a counter-offer from another potential coalition. (NSE/I/GAME THEORY/1285)

(3.4.6) The line-by-line, left-to-right, top-to-bottom dissection and reconstitution of television images is known as scanning. (HTW/I/TELEVISION CAMERA TUBES/120)

(3.4.7) Data available on the thermal conductivity of gases is reliable only within +/- 5% and, therefore, such calculations usually are confined to obtaining a broad estimate of likely sensitivity of an instrument over a limited range of composition. (NSE/I/GAS ANALYZERS/1291)

(3.4.8) ... the majority of effort was devoted to improving turbojet design in the United States... (NSE/I/TURBOPROP ENGINES/66)

(3.4.9) We are accustomed to judging the size or distance of objects by the angle under which we see them... (HTW/I/TELESCOPES/142)

**(4) Adjective + preposition + gerund**

| | |
|---|---|
| **be capable of doing sth** | **etw. tun können** |
| **be incapable of doing sth** | **etw. nicht tun können** |
| **be responsible for doing sth** | **für etw. verantwortlich sein** |
| **be suitable for doing sth** | **sich für etw. eignen** |
| **be resistant to doing sth** | **gegen etw. beständig sein** |
| **be available for doing sth** | **für etw. verfügbar sein** |

Notice that in this construction the preposition is obligatory.

(4.1) **When a process is not capable of working within the tolerances**, either the process or the tolerances must be changed. (NSE/II/STATISTICAL QUALITY CONTROL/2685)
**Wenn ein Arbeitsgang nicht innerhalb der vorgeschriebenen Toleranzen ablaufen kann,** müssen entweder der Arbeitsgang oder die Toleranzen geändert werden.

(4.2) When compared to the other electrical quantities, the var is a relatively new term.... The letters were taken from volt-ampere-reactive and represent power incapable of producing work.
(NSE/I/ELECTRIC POWER AND ENERGY MEASUREMENT/POWER FACTOR /1012)

(4.3) Fertilization, in combination with irrigation, has been responsible for converting vast semiarid and arid lands with lean soils into lands useful for production of a number of important food and fiber crops. (NSE/I/FERTILIZER/1128)

(4.4) Carbon tetrachloride vaporises completely at 76.5°C.... This kind of extinguisher is more particularly suitable for putting out fires in machinery and electrical installations. (HTW/I/FIRE EXTINGUISHERS/10)

(4.5) ... petrol (gasoline) must undergo further chemical processing to give it good anti-knock and ignition properties, reduce its odour, and make it resistant to ageing.
(HTW/I/PETROLEUM DISTILLATION/26)

(4.6) Spraying is the only satisfactory method of deposition available for applying very heavy zinc coatings up to 0.25mm (0.01 in.) and greater in thickness.
(NSE/I/ZINC SPRAYING/1283)

There are a few adjectives that take the gerund immediately after them, e.g. **'worth'**, **'near'**, and **'busy'**:

The values resulting from a series of tests are worth analysing.
The heated liquid is near boiling.
The car mechanic is busy repairing an engine.

### 2.1.4 The Gerund and its Logical Subject

The gerund can be preceded by an item that acts as its logical subject and is different from the grammatical subject of a sentence. The grammatical form of this item determines the nature of the gerund.

The nominal nature of the gerund is due to the use of the **genitive** or **possessive case of a noun** (a) or the **possessive pronoun** (b), each of which functioning grammatically as an attribute with which the gerund forms a close syntactic unit.

The verbal nature of the gerund is due to the use of the **common case of a noun** (c) or the **objective case of a personal pronoun** (d) and **reflexive pronoun** (e) respectively.

Lamprecht (1983, 145-146) points out that within this non-finite construction only a noun in the common case can be taken to be the logical subject of the gerund while the other items are to be interpreted as being merely the 'grammatical carriers' of the logical subject. This type of gerund construction can be regarded as a highly economic substitute for subordinate clauses. It may be related to **nominal clauses**, i.e. mainly object clauses introduced by the conjunction **'that'** (Ge '**daß**'), especially if the preceding verb governs or allows the use of the gerund, or **adverbial clauses** if a preposition precedes the gerund. In this case an alternative to the gerund construction may also be an **infinitive clause**. The respective semantic relationship between a gerund construction, depending on a preposition, and an adverbial clause is based on the same semantic category, such as *contingency, purpose, cause and effect, means and instrument*, etc., which the related structures can denote. Compare the examples given below.

In **SE** instances of the use of the various patterns referred to above vary widely. The analysis on which this book is based resulted in as many as eighteen instances of pattern (c), two instances of pattern (b), and only one instance of pattern (e), whereas no instances of pattern (a) - compare, however, Gerbert (1970, 73) - and pattern (d) could be ascertained. According to these findings, the common case of a noun as logical subject of the gerund shows a high rate of occurrence while all the other patterns seem to be relatively rarely used. This insight into pattern frequency will be considered by the choice of patterns and number of examples given to illustrate the grammatical varieties of the logical subject as follows:

**(1) the noun in the common case;**

**(2) the possessive pronoun in the objective case;**

**(3) the reflexive pronoun in the objective case.**

From an interlingual point of view it must be stressed that the logical subject of the gerund, irrespective of its grammatical form, usually corresponds to the subject of a subordinate clause in Ge.

**(1) The noun in the common case as logical subject of the gerund**

(1.1) The meson theory of nuclear forces, originated by Yukawa, **postulates the atomic nucleus being held together** by an exchange force in which particles, now called mesons, are exchanged between individual nucleons within the nucleus.
(NSE/II/NUCLEAR FORCES/1995)
Die Mesonentheorie von Kernkräften, die von Yukawa aufgestellt wurde, besagt, **daß der Atomkern** von einer Austauschkraft **zusammengehalten wird**, wobei Teilchen, die heute Mesonen genannt werden, zwischen einzelnen Nukleonen innerhalb des Kerns ausgetauscht werden.

Notice the alternative En version:

The meson theory of nuclear forces, originated by Yukawa, **postulates that the atomic nucleus is held together** by an exchange force...

(1.2) If we imagine some action being taken based on the result of a significance test, this action may be referred to as accepting or rejecting the null hypothesis.
(NSE/II/SIGNIFICANCE TESTS/2579)

(1.3) To prevent the energy attaining disastrously high values, resistances are included in the circuit; these cause energy losses in the form of heat.
(HTW/I/RESONANCE(ECHO)/184)

(1.4) **In the event of a connecting hose** between two carriages **rupturing or bursting**, the main brake pipe will lose its air pressure. (HTW/I/PNEUMATIC BRAKE/530)
**Falls ein Verbindungsschlauch** zwischen zwei Eisenbahnwagen **abreißt oder platzt,** entweicht die Druckluft aus der Hauptluftleitung.

Notice two more possibilities of translation:

Für den Fall, daß ein Verbindungsschlauch zwischen zwei Eisenbahnwagen abreißt oder platzt,...
Im Falle des Abreißens oder Platzens eines Verbindungsschlauches zwischen zwei Eisenbahnwagen...

Notice an alternative En version:

**If a connecting hose** between two carriages **ruptures or bursts**, the main brake pipe will lose its air pressure.

(I.5) For aircraft operating over a wide range of speeds and altitudes, such as supersonic jets, some of the control parameters must be changed to reflect new flight environmental conditions. (NSE/I/AUTOMATIC PILOT/287)

Notice the alternative En version:

**For aircraft to operate** over a wide range of speeds and altitudes...

(1.6) At the surface of a liquid, molecules are in a state of dynamic equilibrium... The equilibrium results in the surface layer being constantly less dense than the bulk fluid, which creates a state of tension at the surface. (NSE/I/FOAM/1199)

(1.7) The disappearance of the colloidal state of a substance may be accomplished in either of two directions, namely by the colloid passing into solution or into suspension. (NSE/I/COLLOID SYSTEM/CONDENSATION PROCESSES/700)

**(2) The possessive pronoun in the objective case as logical subject of the gerund**

(2.1) If a material is subjected to an alternating stress (such as a spring which is repeatedly and rapidly being compressed and released, and then compressed again), slip occurs in the actual particles of the material itself, **which results in its having a very much lower elastic limit**. (OJE/VIII/ENGINEERING DESIGN/138)

... wenn ein metallischer Werkstoff einer Wechselbeanspruchung unterworfen wird, (wie zum Beispiel eine Feder, die wiederholt und schnell zusammengedrückt wird), tritt in den eigentlichen Werkstoffteilchen Gleiten auf, **was dazu führt, daß seine Elastizitätsgrenze deutlich sinkt.**

(2.2) In the Apollo capsule and in future earth-orbiting space stations the crew will live in less cramped conditions and enjoy greater comfort, more particularly because they will be able to remove their cumbersome outer suits inside the cabin. This is possible because these spacecraft are of double-wall construction, with intermediate layers of rubberlike material which are self-sealing in the event of their being punctured by meteorites, so that no sudden loss of pressure within the capsule will occur. (HTW/II/SPACE SUITS AND SPACE CAPSULES/372)

**(3) The reflexive pronoun in the objective case as logical subject of the gerund**

(3.1) Soldering is the process of joining metal parts by means of a molten filler metal (solder) whose melting point is lower than that of the metals to be joined. The latter are wetted by the molten filler **without themselves being melted** (as in welding). (HTW/ II/SOLDERING/138)

Löten ist ein Verfahren zum Vereinigen von metallischen Teilen mit Hilfe eines geschmolzenen Zusatzmetalls (Lot), dessen Schmelztemperatur niedriger ist als diejenige der zu vereinigenden Metalle. Die letzteren werden von dem geschmolzenen Lot benetzt, **ohne selbst geschmolzen zu werden** (wie beim Schweißen).

### 2.1.5 The Gerund as a Constituent Part of Compounds

In term formation the gerund has turned out to be one of the most productive categories for nominal compounds, which are formed by combining two or more words into a new syntagmatic unit with a new meaning independent of the constituent parts. "Most new terms are formed as and when new concepts are created in such instances as new discoveries, restructuring of existing knowledge, incidental observations or planned industrial developments. In each of these cases the new concept to be named is seen in a particular light in relation to other concepts around it. It is therefore not surprising that the linguistic sign for a concept can be quite arbitrarily chosen and often is" (Sager 1990, 62). The gerund, however, has been deliberately used for the building of terminological systems. There are, for example, two outstanding patterns of term creation in which it occurs as either the **first element (determinant)** or **second element (nucleus)** of a compound and in various functions, i.e. the first element determines what is expressed by the second, while the syntactic-semantic relationship between the two varies greatly.

The kind of relationship can be made transparent by the operation of '**definition by paraphrase**', exemplified, for example, in a thorough analysis of terms in the field of **metal forming** (Baakes, 1984). Compare the examples listed below which show that compounds are based on various syntagmatic structures, which in turn are due to the rules governing the grammatical arrangement of words in sentences.

The nature of the gerund varies according to its function and place in a compound.

(1) Its nominal nature is evident when the gerund functions as the second element or nucleus, e.g.

| En | ***syntactic-semantic relationship*** | Ge |
|---|---|---|
| metal forming | techniques of **the forming of metals** | Umformtechnik |

(2) Its verbal nature is preserved when the gerund functions as the first element or determinant, which, however, does not necessarily imply that the respective 'semantic-syntactic relationship' can be used to show this.

Compare the following examples:

| En | *syntactic-semantic relationship* | Ge |
|---|---|---|
| forming equipment | **equipment** used **for forming** a workpiece | Umformmaschinen |
| forming speed | the **speed** of changing the workpiece **during forming** | Umform-geschwindigkeit |
| forming force | the **force** acting between the tools which is **necessary for the deformation** of the workpiece | Umformkraft |
| forming work | the **work** done **in forming** a workpiece/ the **work necessary for a deformation** | Umformarbeit |
| forming temperature | the **temperature at which the deformation** of the workpiece **occurs** | Umformtemperatur |
| forming resistance | **resistance** of a material **to change of shape** | Umformwiderstand |
| forming limit | the **ability** of a metal **to deform without fracture** | Umformgrenze |

Since these compounds are terms, which "are the linguistic representation of concepts" (Sager 1990, 57), it is only the gerund as determinant that takes stress as distinct from the formally identical free collocation consisting of **present participle plus noun** where both elements take a strong stress (level stress). A further point of distiction is that the present participle can be expanded into a relative clause. Compare:

| **ab'sorbing well** | **ab'sorbing 'liquid** |
|---|---|
| Ge Sickerschacht (für Grundwasser) | Ge absorbierende Flüssigkeit |
| Definition:<br><br>A shaft sunk through an impermeable stratum to allow water to drain through to a permeable one. | Context:<br><br>The absorption medium is a liquid in which (1) the gas to be removed, i.e. absorbed is soluble in the liquid, or (2) a chemical reaction takes place between the gas and the absorbing liquid. |
| (CHAMBERS 1988, 3 / HYDRAULIC ENGINEERING - Ge WASSERBAU) | (NSE/I/ABSORPTION(PROCESS)/6)<br>**Note**: a liquid that is absorbing (the gas) |

Mention must also be made that the elements of noun compounds are often joined by a hyphen. Unfortunately, there are no strict rules for the use of hyphens and, as far as scientific and technical noun compounds are concerned, a relatively great number of them are not hyphenated except noun compounds composed of more than two elements, where there may be the risk of misunderstanding. Swales (1971, 131) refers to the well-known example **small car factory** which could mean either:

**a small factory for making cars**
**a factory for making small cars.**

If the second alternative is meant the compound should be written: **a small-car factory**.
Long compounds such as

| | | |
|---|---|---|
| **low-pressure die-casting** | **(foundry)** | **Ge Niederdruck-Kokillenguß** |
| **quick-change turning-tool holder** | **(metal cutting)** | **Ge Schnellwechsel-Drehmeißelhalter** |

are sometimes difficult to understand if they are encountered for the first time. However, they are not always as difficult as they look if, in an attempt to interpret such compounds, this principle is followed: Begin at the end and then work backwards.
The steps to be taken to understand **quick-change turning-tool holder**, for instance, are:

What is the last word? ...

Therefore, the most important thing is that it has the function of holding or supporting something.

What is the next to the last word? ...

Therefore, it has the function of holding the turning-tool.

What is the last word from the end? ...

Therefore, it can be inferred that this sort of holder allows a quick change of the turning-tool. When still in doubt, the result of this procedure can be followed up by a careful study of a text whose context is related to it, e.g.

> "Once **the tools are set in their appropriate toolholders, they can be quickly changed** and still maintain the setting accuracy" (Black 1981, 166).

**2.1.6 The Multiple Use of the Gerund**

In **SE** the gerund is extensively used for the purpose of

**(1)** expressing **sequential phases in a process,**

**(2)** establishing a relation between noun phrases, known as **apposition,**

**(3)** indicating **purpose**, and

**(4)** representing **conceptual relationships.**

**(1) The gerund used to express sequential phases in a process**

(1.1) A complete cycle of operations comprises **closing the die, forcing the molten metal into it, withdrawing the cores, opening the die, ejecting the casting** and (if necessary) **shearing off the sprue, deburring the casting,** and **cleaning the die**.
(HTW/II/PRESSURE DIE CASTING/110)

(1.2) The mild soap is made **by drying a good grade of neat soap** to about 15% moisture content, **breaking up the crystalline structure** that develops **during drying and cooling, plasticising and converting a sufficient portion of the soap to a desirable phase condition, deaerating and compacting the** resulting **mass, and forming it into bars.** (NSE/II/SOAPS/ MILD BAR SOAP MANUFACTURE/2611)

(1.3) The inverter offers **the possibility of generating power** as alternating current, then **stepping it up to the desired transmission voltage, rectifying it** with high-efficiency rectifiers, **transmitting as high-voltage direct current** with certain advantages, **inverting it to alternating current** at the receiving end, and **stepping it down to the normal distribution voltage by using transformers.** (NSE/I/INVERTER/1589)

**(2) Gerunds used in apposition**

Appositions show a variety of semantic relationships between noun phrases, such as **exemplification** (2.1) and **identification** (2.2).

(2.1) **Exemplification**

In exemplification the gerund is used as the second appositive to exemplify the reference of the more general term in the first appositive. Explicit indicators are: **'for example'**, **'e.g.'**, **'including'**, **'such as'**.

Sheet-metal work usually starts with a **basic preliminary operation such as cutting, slitting, perforating, etc.**, performed with tools that exercise a shearing action.
(HTW/II/SHEET-METAL WORK/140)

(2.2) **Identification**

In identification the gerund is used as the second appositive to identify what is referred to by the less specific noun phrase forming the first appositive. Hence the optional indicator **'namely'** may be inserted.

> There are **two general methods of prestressing, namely pretensioning and post-tensioning**. (NSE/II/PRESTRESSED CONCRETE/2311)

**(3) Gerunds used to indicate purpose**

> Modern chromatography plays three major roles in science and industry, separately or in combination: (1) As **a means for identifying and quantifying the ingredients of a mixture** of chemical substances - as used in the laboratory for quality control, for example, **detecting impurities** in chemicals, pharmaceuticals, foodstuffs, etc.; **assisting researchers** in the study of biochemistry; **measuring and identifying unsafe materials** in the environment; and as an aid in forensic science, among scores of other specific applications. (NSE/I/CHROMATOGRAPHY/625)

**(4) Gerunds used to represent conceptual relationships**

Gerunds are used to represent **generic relationships** (4.1) and **partitive relationships** (4.2) which in a given text are linguistically linked by verbs such as **subdivide into, include**, etc.

(4.1) "The **generic relationship** establishes a hierarchical order; it identifies concepts as belonging to the same category in which there is a broader (generic) concept which is said to be superordinate to the narrower (specific), subordinated concept or concepts" (Sager 1990, 30).
Compare:

> The most important and most widely used fusion-welding technique is **arc welding... The general technique can be subdivided** into three categories: **open-arc welding, covered-arc welding, and gas-shielded arc welding.**
> (HTW/II/FUSION WELDING/134)

(4.2) The **partitive relationships** "serve to indicate the connection between concepts consisting of more than one part and their constituent parts" (ibidem 32).

> **Beneficiation**. This is **a term which describes all processes used to improve the chemical and physical characteristics of ore** (not limited to iron ore) for later use. In the case of iron ore, beneficiation makes the ore better for handling by the blast furnace. **The principal methods include crushing, screening, blending, grinding, concentrating, classifying, and agglomerating.**
> (NSE/I/IRON ORE PROCESSING/BENEFICIATION/1601)

## 2.2 Participial Constructions

### 2.2.1 Forms and Basic Functions of Participles

#### (1) Formation and meanings of simple participles

There are two simple participles, the **present participle** and the **past participle.** The present participle ends in **-ing**, the past participle ends in **-ed** in the case of regular verbs, whereas in the case of irregular verbs the third principal part is the past participle. Compare:

| Present Participle | Past Participle |
|---|---|
| **working** | **worked** (regular verb) |
| **driving** | **driven** (irregular verb) |

The difference between the two is that the present participle construction usually has an active meaning and refers to the continuation of an action, whereas the past participle has a passive one (a) and often refers to the result of an action in the case of transitive verbs (b). Compare:

| Present Participle | Past Participle |
|---|---|
| He **kept** the engine **running**.<br>(=the engine **was running. Active**)<br>Ge Er **ließ** den Motor **laufen**. | (a) A force **called** thrust...<br>(=A force **which is called** thrust... **Passive**)<br>Ge Eine Kraft, **die** Schub **genannt wird**.<br>(b) A coil spring **keeps** the choke **closed**.<br>(=the choke **is closed**)<br>Ge Eine Wickelfeder **hält** die Starterklappe **geschlossen**. |

Intransitive verbs whose past participle is active, such as "faded colour = the colour that has faded", are negligible.

It should be noted that the terms **'present'** and **'past'** may be misleading since the present participle does not necessarily signify any time at all, nor does the past participle invariably refer to an *action or state* in the past, i.e. both forms can give up their verbal function and become adjectives, which, like any other conventional adjectives, are used to describe the *thing, quality, state,* or *action* which a noun refers to.

Furthermore, the passive meaning of the past participle has been shown to vary between an *action* and a *resulting state,* depending on whether the underlying passive construction is an **actional passive** or a **statal passive.**

"In the actional passive **be** is an auxillary, the past participle is head of the VP and - provided there is a **by** phrase complement of the appropriate kind - the clause can be straightforwardly related to an active counterpart... In the statal passive, the **be** is a main verb, head of the VP predicator, while the past participle functions as (head of) a predicative complement, and there is no equivalent transformational derivation" (Huddleston 1984, 322). In other words, the actional passive says that a certain event takes place in which case the past participle is unmistakably a verb, while a statal passive attributes a certain property to the respective noun in which case the past participle functions as a noun qualifier and is to be analysed as an adjective. Despite this grammatical difference, the fact remains that the formal identity of the two structures often gives rise to some difficulty of interpretation.

Sager/Dungworth (1980, 1086) exemplify this problem as follows: "The past participle can be used as an attributive and a predicative adjective as well as in purely verbal functions. Its verbal character is more clearly in evidence in postmodification of a noun and in predicative function where, in fact, it is difficult to differentiate it from the passive, cf.

| | |
|---|---|
| *process* : | The input is held constant above a specific level. |
| *result of process* : | Thus a high overall sensitivity is achieved. |
| *state* : | A thermometer-type tuning indicator is fitted." |

**(2) The formation of continuous tenses**

One of the important basic functions of the present participle is to form, with various parts of the auxiliary verb '**be**', the **continuous tenses.**

Compare:

The liquid wets the surface on which **it is condensing.**

In general English the continuous form of the verb is considered a valuable tool of expression, which plays a great role in modifying utterances stylistically. In the relatively objective and matter-of-fact language of scientists and engineers, however, it has primarily the function of referring to the incompleteness and continuation of an action, although it can occasionally be found in contexts where the emphasis is on the *present moment* or where *progressive change* or *habitual actions* are to be indicated. Compared to the frequency of occurrence of other verb forms, such as the passive verbs, the continuous form of the verb is most sparingly used in **SE**.

In German there is no construction available that can be compared with the continuous form of the verb. For that reason the various parts of the continuous tenses are to be translated into German just in the same way as any other simple form of tense is, with adverbs of time being usually added, such as "gerade", "in diesem Augenblick", etc. The following examples show the use of three continuous tenses in the active and passive voice of which the present tense is obviously the commonest in **SE**.

**Present Continuous Tense (Active)**

Computer simulation **is playing** an increasing role in such research...
(NSE/I/DRAG STUDIES IN THE AUTOMOTIVE FIELD/49)

**Present Continuous Tense (Passive)**

While the piston **is being forced** in one direction by the expanding steam, the spent steam is pushed out of the cylinder on the other side of the cylinder.
(HTW/I/STEAM ENGINE/38)

**Present Perfect Continuous Tense (Active)**

Several organisations **have been working** on the standards problem for a number of years... (NSE/II/LOCAL AREA NETWORKS/COMMON STANDARDS/ 1728)

**Past Continuous Tense (Passive)**

In the early 1960s over 80% of this mixture **was still being produced** from solid fuels. At the present time, however, processes for making synthesis gas from natural gas and hydrocarbons are gaining ground.
(HTW/II/SYNTHESIS GAS AND METHANOL SYNTHESIS/42)

**(3) The formation of perfect tenses**

The past participle is used to form, with various parts of the auxiliary verb **'have'**, the **perfect tenses**, such as the **present perfect tense** illustrated by the following examples:

Experience **has shown** that... (Active)

It **has been found** that... (Passive)

Note that the present perfect tense, although it indicates an action that took place in the past, is associated with the **present** idea of **now.**

**(4) The formation of the passive voice**

The past participle is used to form, with various parts of the auxiliary verb **'be'**, the **passive voice.** Compare:

> One type of electrostatic generator **is known** as a Van de Graaff generator in which a moving belt **is charged** by a low-voltage supply, such as a battery, and this charge **is deposited** onto a hollow, spherically shaped shell, on which a voltage **can be developed** that is 100 times or more the voltage of the primary supply, depending on the radius of the shell and the electric field at which voltage breakdown occurs.
> (NSE/I/ELECTROSTATIC GENERATOR/1049)

Remember that "known" is an adjective (refer back to sections 2.1.2/(3) and (3.4)), whereas "is charged", "is deposited", and "can be developed" are verbal passive forms.

As stated in section 1.2, scientists and engineers are used to impersonal and objective communication when dealing with their subject matter. That explains the frequent use of the **passive** in **SE**. Gerbert (1970, 87) points out that "neben der stark ausgeprägten Tendenz zu nominalen Fügungen gilt der häufige Gebrauch des Passivs als bezeichnendstes Merkmal des wissenschaftlichen Stils." Swales (1971, 39) assumes that "in any physics, chemistry, or engineering text-book at least one-third of all the finite verbs will be in the passive. Most of these passive verbs will be either in the Present Simple or be used with modals like **will, can, may** or **should.**"

Sager/Dungworth (1980, 1084) give the following lucid explanation for the dominating role of the passive in **SE**: "Technical language is characterised by the impersonal use of verbs, and in particular the avoidance of first and second person pronouns. In English this is largely achieved by the use of the passive, in fact to a greater extent than in German which can alternate the passive with a larger number of impersonal verbs, with various reflexive verbs and with the impersonal pronoun **"man"...** The only other way of expressing impersonal statements is by constructions like: **it is possible/likely/desirable that...** and **it appears/seems/proves/becomes possible/necessary/inevitable that ...**

The passive is also used to avoid stylistically unacceptable repetition of the covered subject where a whole series of actions is carried out by the same person(s), for example **I, we, the experimenter, the authors.** The choice of the passive enables attention to be focussed on the effect or the result of the action. In English particularly, the position of the grammatical subject early in the clause gives it a special prominence and scientists and technologists tend to concentrate information in it."

**(5) The formation of compound participles**

In addition to the simple participles discussed above, there are three compound ones. These comprise

(a) the **present passive participle**, formed by **being + a past participle**,

(b) the **perfect participle active**, formed by **having + a past participle**, and

(c) the **perfect participle passive**, formed by **having been + a past participle**.

Compare the following examples:

(a) **The plant being built** will be used for the production of petrol.
**Die Anlage, die gebaut wird,** wird für die Herstellung von Benzin genutzt werden.

(b) **Having located the leak, the mechanics** were able to restore the purification system to full working order.
**Nachdem die Industriemechaniker die undichte Stelle ausfindig gemacht hatten,** konnten sie die vollständige Betriebsfähigkeit der Kläranlage wiederherstellen.

(c) **All the problems having been resolved,** the engineers put the new plant on trial.
**Nachdem alle Probleme gelöst worden waren,** ließen die Ingenieure die neue Anlage probeweise laufen.

Note that the perfect participle refers to an action that took place before the time expressed by the main verb.

**(6) Survey of forms and meanings of the participles**

| | PRESENT PARTICIPLE | PERFECT PARTICIPLE | PAST PARTICIPLE |
|---|---|---|---|
| **Active:** | forming | having formed | |
| **Passive:** | being formed | having been formed | formed |
| **Meaning(s):** | *simultaneity* | *anteriority* | *simultaneity or anteriority* |
| **Ge** | *Gleichzeitigkeit* | *Vorzeitigkeit* | |

### 2.2.2 Present Participle Constructions

#### 2.2.2.1 Premodification of a Noun

The present participle has some characteristics in common with the adjective: It can function as a noun qualifier and as such can be used attributively. Moreover, it can be modified by an adverb. Compare:

(1) In water turbines the kinetic energy of **flowing** or **falling water** is converted into mechanical rotary motion. (HTW/I/WATER TURBINES/44)
In Wasserturbinen wird die kinetische Energie von **strömendem** oder **fallendem Wasser** in mechanische Rotationsbewegung umgewandelt.

(2) There are seemingly limitless related compounds of differing molecular size and constitution which incorporate varying kinds and numbers of functional groups. (NSE/I/CHEMICAL NATURE OF AMINO ACIDS/124)

(3) Fire extinguishing agents must therefore either cool the combustible material, or they must cover this material with a **firmly adhering non-inflammable coating...** (HTW/I/FIRE EXTINGUISHERS/10)

(4) On leaving the impeller, the fluid may first pass through a ring of fixed vanes which surrounds the impeller and is known as a diffuser. In this device with its gradually widening passages the velocity of the liquid is reduced... (HTW/I/PUMPS/20)

#### 2.2.2.2 Postmodification of a Noun

As unexpanded postmodifiers the present active participle and the present passive one occur in different frequency. The postposition of the former (1) is very rare, whereas the latter (2) is quite common in this position. Due to their position the participles have clearly verbal quality.

(1) The active participle allows of two possibilities of translation into German:

as a relative clause (a) and as a premodifying participle (b). Compare:

(1.1) The shaft eccentricity meter will automatically indicate and record **the amount of eccentricity existing.**

(a) Der Wellenexzentrizitätsmesser zeigt automatisch **den Betrag der Exzentrizität an, der vorhanden ist,** und registriert ihn.

(b) Der Wellenexzentrizitätsmesser zeigt automatisch **den vorhandenen Betrag der Exzentrizität an...**

(1.2) Some authorities believe that the physical principles of the modular high-temperature gas-cooled reactor have been amply proved. Thus, the basic problems remaining relate to building hardware at a reduced capital cost...
(NSE/II/NUCLEAR POWER/SECOND-GENERATION HTGRs/ 2009)

(2) The passive participle can only be translated as a passive relative clause into German:

(2.1) Very high cutting speeds would, in the absence of cooling, cause excessive heating of **the surface being drilled,** in as much as the tooth material is a poor conductor of heat.
(HTW/II/HIGH-SPEED TURBINE DRILL/402)
Sehr hohe Bohrgeschwindigkeiten würden bei fehlender Kühlung eine zu starke Erwärmung der **Oberfläche, die gebohrt wird,** verursachen, da das Zahnmaterial ein schlechter Wärmeleiter ist.

(2.2) A simple and common method is known as resistance coupling. This is coupling in which resistors are used as the input and output impedances of the circuits being coupled. (NSE/I/AMPLIFIER/139)

(2.3) The liquid being measured flows continuously into and out of the vessel by way of flexible connections.
(NSE/II/SPECIFIC GRAVITY/BALANCED-FLOW VESSEL/2655)

(2.4) The tap between the rolls is less than the height (thickness) of the material being rolled.
(NSE/I/ROLLING/1611)

### 2.2.2.3 Inversion in Declarative Sentences

Sager et al. (1980, 189) refer to the fact that "Subject - Predicate inversion is comparatively rare in **SE** except for certain participial or adjectival phrases used with the connective **be** which often appear in initial position in descriptive statements." Compare the following examples which **show** the fronting of **the present participle** as **predicate:**

(1) The cellular structure in leaves is very constant. **Covering the entire surface of the leaf is the epidermis,** a layer of tabular cells... **Occupying all the rest of the leaf is a loose tissue** composed of irregularly arranged rounded cells known as the spongy mesophyll. (NSE/II/LEAF/1690)

Die Zellstruktur in Blättern ist sehr gleichmäßig. **Die Epidermis,** eine Schicht tabellenförmiger Zellen, **bedeckt die gesamte Oberfläche des Blattes**... **Ein lockeres Gewebe,** das sich aus unregelmäßig geordneten runden Zellen zusammensetzt, die als lockeres Mesophyll bekannt sind, **nimmt den Rest des Blattes ein.**

(2) Most noticeable is that the peaks of the spectrum are broadened to a greater or lesser extent by the characteristics of the devices used to detect gamma rays. Relating to this broadening as a measure of system quality, is its "resolution". This is a function both of the detector and of the associated circuitry.
(NSE/I/GAMMA-RAY SPECTROSCOPY/1287)

(3) Milling machines are of the horizontal or the vertical type. A commonly employed horizontal machine is the knee type... Projecting from the front of the column is the knee, whose top surface carries the saddle. (HTW/II/MILLING MACHINE/186)

Sentence structures like these are said to be common in journalism where "the fronting of the predication seems largely determined in fact by the desire to give end-focus to the subject, at the same time using (as is normal) the early part of the sentence 'to set the scene'" (Quirk et al. 1985, 1379). In the Special Languages of Science and Technology, however, the use of participles at the head of inverted predicates allows of a more rational explanation, which Sager et al. (ibidem) give by drawing upon Gerbert's interpretation. Thus they state: "His own explanation is that inversion has the advantage of permitting direct modification of the subject by several attributive or relative clauses as, for example, in the description of the technical details of machines, engines and equipment. The usual S-P sequence would lead to overloading of the subject and make the sentence top-heavy, whereas inversion relieves the reader of the necessity of mentally storing up too much information before the predicate appears. This kind of inversion can therefore be classified as one of the syntactic devices which **SE** has taken over from general English and adapted to suit its special communicative needs."

Gerbert's list of present participles commonly encountered in initial position as inverted predicates includes: **supporting, extending, protruding, projecting, encircling, embracing, sliding, working, and operating** (cf. Gerbert 1960, 61).

The sample sentences given above suggest considerable scope for the use of this type of syntactic construction and substantiate the view that the use of participles as inverted predicates indeed meets the specific needs of **SE** communication.

#### 2.2.2.4 The Present Participle as Complement of a Clause Element

**(1) The present participle as predicative subject complement**

In **SE** one type of participle construction used in this function is particularly noteworthy: the **participle construction of characterization** preceded by **as** and used in **passive sentences.** As its name indicates, it characterizes, or partly identifies, the antecedent noun to which it refers. In the introduction to his thorough analysis of this construction, Meier (1990, 73) points out that "the participles preceded by **as** can be considered to constitute an important construction of English as a written language. Yet though they occur with relative frequency, they have been neglected in grammars, where either no mention is made of them at all or where they are dealt with in passing." He classifies the verbs that take the participle construction of characterization according to semantic criteria as follows:

(a) verbs of *judgement/opinion* and *perception*, e.g.

**recognize, perceive, conceive, consider;**

(b) verbs of *statement* and *description*, e.g.

**explain, describe, report;**

(c) verbs of *offering, acceptance* and *rejection*, e.g

**accept, dismiss.**

(1.1) **The present active participle as subject complement**

(1.1.1) **Three basic stages are** generally **recognized as occurring** during the annealing of cold worked metals. These are recovery, recrystallization, and grain growth. (NSE/I/ANNEALING/167)

Im allgemeinen **ist anerkannt, daß** während des Glühens kaltumgeformter Metalle **drei Grundstufen auftreten.** Diese umfassen Erholung, Rekristallisation und Kornwachstum.

(1.1.2) For a given accoustic pressure, sounds differing in pitch are not perceived as having the same loudness. (HTW/I/ELECTRIC HORN/518)

(1.1.3) Iron (or steel) can be conceived as consisting of numerous randomly disposed magnetic units, or domains, which cancel one another so that the piece of metal as a whole exhibits no magnetic polarity. (HTW/II/ELECTROMAGNETS/502)

(1.2) **The present passive participle as subject complement**

(1.2.1) In an electric field **all points** having the same voltage **are conceived as being connected** by so-called equipotential lines. (HTW/I/ELECTRON MICROSCOPE/140)
**Man stellt sich vor, daß** in einem elektrischen Feld **alle Punkte**, die die gleiche Spannung haben, durch sogenannte Äquipotentiallinien **miteinander verbunden sind.**

(1.2.2) The other and most commonly used concept in determining propeller performance is the blade element theory. In this theory (known as the Drzewiecki theory), each propeller blade is considered as being composed of an infinite number of air foils (called blade elements) joined end to end, forming a shape similar to a twisted airplane wing. (NSE/I/PROPELLERS/63)

(1.2.3) With the planetarium instrument it is also possible to demonstrate the precessional motion of the earth's axis, or "precession of the equinoxes", a phenomenon already known in ancient times and subsequently explained by Newton as being caused by the equatorial bulge (or the flattened shape of the poles) of the earth. (HTW/II/PLANETARIUM/396)

(1.3) Other verbs taking the **present participle as subject complement** include **remain** (used in the active voice), **show** as well as *durative* **keep** and *causative* **set.** Compare:

(1.3.1) A very fine synthetic powder (called the toner) with special frictional electric properties is mixed with small steel and quartz balls provided with a coating of special plastic. ... If a mixture of this kind is moved about on the coated plate, **particles** at first adhering to the carrier balls are detached from these and **remain adhering to the** more highly charged **areas of the plate.**
(HTW/I/COPYING AND DUPLICATING(XEROGRAPHIC METHOD)/424)

Two small groups of verbs, namely **lie, sit, stand** as well as **go** and **come**, which are also used in the active voice, can hardly be expected in **SE**.

(1.3.2) **The cathodes** of the main lamp **are kept glowing** at white heat by the impingement of positive mercury ions, and the lamp thus continues to function and emit light in the manner described. (HTW/I/ FLUORESCENT LAMP/100)

(1.3.3) **The two flows are shown covering the same region** in Fig.20.
(NSE/ I/THEORY OF AERODYNAMIC CIRCULATION/52)

(1.3.4) In Fig.1 a neutron is shown hitting a nucleus of uranium 235. **The latter is set vibrating** as a result of this impact... (HTW/I/NUCLEAR REACTOR/50)

Note that the following example shows the extremely rare use of the **perfect participle** as subject complement:

> More recently, **the jet has been explained as having been ejected** from the nucleus of the galaxy in one or a series of explosions about a million years prior to the state that is presently being observed from earth. (NSE/II/ELLIPTICAL GALAXIES/1276)

**(2) The present participle as predicative object complement**

Unlike the majority of verbs which occur in the passive when used with the present participle as subject complement, the verbs used with the present participle as object complement usually occur in the active. Compare:

(2.1) **The participle construction of characterization**

(2.1.1) After wind tunnel tests, development was discontinued because of the economic depression and scientific reluctance **to accept the engine as having any practical significance.** (NSE/I/TURBOPROP ENGINES/66)
Nach Versuchen im Windkanal wurde die Entwicklung wegen der wirtschaftlichen Depression und der Ablehnung der Wissenschaft, **das Triebwerk als bedeutsam für die Praxis zu akzeptieren,** eingestellt.

(2.1.2) The photocells are interconnected so that each single cell "sees" not only its own portion of the character being read, but also the portions covered by other cells around it. This arrangement enables the device to judge relationships, dismiss smudges as not being part of the characters, and accept even the light portion of the character because the area next to the character is even lighter.
(NSE/II/OPTICAL CHARACTER RECOGNITION (OCR)/2080)

(2.1.3) The aforementioned researchers have reported that lithium-sodium beta alumina as having a lithium/sodium ratio greater than about 1 and thus appears to be the first generally useful lithium superionic conductor reported thus far. It is described as exhibiting strikingly nonlinear ion exchange properties and thus may presage the discovery of similar co-ionic interaction in other superionic conductors.
(NSE/II/LITHIUM/1721)

(2.2) Other verbs taking the **present participle as object complement** include *durative* **keep** and verbs of *perception.* Compare:

(2.2.1) **The water flow controller keeps the water flowing** at the desired pre-set rate by throttling down the main pressure.
(HTW/I/GASFIRED WATER HEATER (GEYSER)/248)

**Der Wasserstromregler läßt das Wasser** durch Drosseln des Hauptdruckes in der gewünschten voreingestellten Geschwindigkeit **strömen.**

(2.2.2) Once the locomotive is in motion, the torque required to keep it going is less and the amount of electric power consumed is accordingly reduced.
(HTW/I/ELECTRIC LOCOMOTIVE/10)

(2.2.3) Magnesium generally has not been considered a major factor in bone formation and strength, but recent studies suggest closer attention be given to dietary levels of magnesium in this regard. Because of the close interrelationship with calcium, it is not surprising to see research findings of magnesium interfering with calcium entry into cells of the islets of the pancreas in studies of diabetes.
(NSE/II/MAGNESIUM(IN BIOLOGICAL SYSTEMS)/1759)

The ascertained sample sentences do not show the use of the present passive participle; nor do they contain important verbs, such as **get (sth) going, leave,** and **set** with the meaning **'veranlassen (zu)'** as well as **have** with the meanings **'(zu)lassen; veranlassen'** and **find,** which also may take the present participle as object complement. As far as their role in **SE** is concerned, further research into this kind of usage is certainly necessary; suffice it to say that their place in **SE** is not called into question, although it may turn out to be less prominent (cf. also section 2.4.2). Notice that, whenever the basic structure consists of **predicate** (verb of any of the semantic classes mentioned) + **object** + **participle** (as object complement), the grammatical object is, strictly speaking, the 'logical' subject of the participle, if the latter is conceived as a finite verb functioning as predicate.

This can be made plain by an analysis of the relatively simple structure of the following sentence extracted from Lamprecht (1970, 293):

We find the <u>same scientific</u> words **being used** in several languages.

We find the <u>same scientific words</u>.

<u>The same scientific words are</u> used in several languages.

The translation of the participial construction into German is suggested as follows:

Wir **stellen fest, daß** die gleichen Fachausdrücke in verschiedenen Sprachen **verwendet werden.**

Knowledge of the syntactic relationship and its underlying logical principle provides important clues to the correct interpretation of this type of participial construction.

#### 2.2.2.5 The Present Participle as Relative Clause Equivalent

The present participle is extensively made use of as a means of reducing **relative clauses** and thus contributes largely to the concise quality of scientific and technical writing. The reduction of an active relative clause consists in omitting the relative pronoun **(which, etc.)** and changing the verb to a present participle. Compare:

(1) **Operations which involve the mixing of solid, liquid and gaseous substances** occur in innumerable industrial manufacturing processes.
**Operations involving the mixing of solid, liquid and gaseous substances** occur in innumerable industrial manufacturing processes.
(HTW/II/MIXING OF MATERIALS/498)

In German two versions are also possible. Notice, however, that the German participle can only be used attributively, preceding the noun.

**Die das Mischen von festen, flüssigen und gasförmigen Substanzen beinhaltenden Arbeitsgänge** kommen in zahllosen industriellen Fertigungsverfahren vor.

Mention should also be made that the German participial construction is often felt to be stilted and not conducive to a clear understanding. The alternative is the version with a relative clause:

**Arbeitsgänge, die das Mischen von festen, flüssigen und gasförmigen Substanzen beinhalten**, kommen in zahllosen industriellen Fertigungsverfahren vor.

Note, too, that the German present participle is functionally much more restricted and consequently has a much lower frequency of occurrence.

It must be emphasized that English present participles expanded into postmodifying clauses should not a priori be seen as abbreviated progressive forms in relative clauses. In **SE** many *stative* verbs, for instance, which cannot have the progressive form in the finite verb phrase, are used in participial form. These verbs usually refer to a *state* (i.e. an *unchanging condition*), for example **have** (indicating *possession*), **be** (whose complements indicate *permanent character istics*), **contain, consist of, depend on,** etc., and thus differ from *dynamic* verbs which can be used in the progressive aspect.

The following example shows the use of the *dynamic* verb **move** and the *stative*-like verb **result from** (indicating *consequence*), which is not normally used in the continuous tenses.

Compare:

(2) It has been found...that the flow pattern about **a body moving through the air at high speeds** is affected to a large degree by **changes in density resulting from compression or expansion of the fluid.**
(NSE/I/THEORY OF AERODYNAMIC COMPRESSIBILITY/49)

Syntactic alternatives are:

**(which is moving)**
**(which result from;** not: *which are resulting from)

The tense to be attributed to the participial clause will usually be that of the finite clause in which the noun phrase (e.g. 'a body moving through the air') occurs, especially if the noun phrase is object (like 'body'), or it is to be inferred from the context.

(3) ... the kinetic energy of the fission products accounts for 160 MeV. These fragments being of significantly lower atomic number, require fewer neutrons for stability than they actually contain immediately after fission. (NSE/I/BINDING ENERGY/359)

(4) Some galvanized sheets are annealed after dipping in order to form a coating consisting entirely of iron-zinc compounds, a process which tends to increase resistance to peeling. (NSE/I/HOT-DIP GALVANIZING/1283)

The use of the present active participle and the present passive one in the same sentence, which is not uncommon in **SE**, is illustrated by the following example:

(5) Traditionally, an alloy has been defined as **a substance having metallic properties and being composed of two or more chemical elements** of which at least one is a metal. (NSE/I/ALLOYS/97)

Note that there are no reduced forms of active relative clauses which contain modal verbs, such as **may, can,** etc. The reason for this is obvious. "If modal verbs are used to give extra meaning to the verb, then this extra meaning will be lost again in a reduced clause" (Swales 1971,61).

The following example indicates that use is also made of **verbless clauses** in which an adverb occurs with the defining appositive:

(6) Geological and geochemical analysis indicates that these meteorites formed inside parent bodies resembling **asteroids, typically some hundreds of kilometers in diameter,** about 4.5 billion years ago. (NSE/II/CLASSES OF METEORITES/1833)

This construction, which can be made more transparent by inserting the present participle **being,** viz. "**asteroids, typically being some hundreds of kilometers in diameter**", is a special type of reduced relative clauses. Without reduction the relative clause shows this structure :

"**asteroids, which are typically some hundreds of kilometers in diameter**".

So far the present participle has been discussed as a device for reducing relative clauses, which are also called **adnominal relative clauses** because they have a **noun phrase** as antecedent. Unlike this type of relative clauses, the **sentential relative clause** refers back to the predicate or predication of a clause or to a whole clause or sentence and is commonly introduced by the relative pronoun **'which'** = Ge **'was'**. But, again, it is its reduced version that is generally preferred. Thus the relatively frequent occurrence of reduced sentential relative clauses or final **-ing** clauses of result, as they are also called, can be regarded as another feature of **SE** syntax. Reduced relative clauses of this type are used to denote the *result* of the action expressed by the main clause, its force often being reinforced by the insertion of the word **'thus'** = Ge **'so'** or **'thereby'** = Ge **'dadurch'** in front of the present participle. The underlying ***syntactic-semantic relationship*** of *cause and effect* explains Swales (1971, 106) thus: "**X** happens, causing **y** to happen". He points out that "such **-ing** clauses are particularly useful in descriptions of how things work, because with them we can avoid describing a series of events using a series of 'ands': **x** happens, and **y** happens, and then **z** happens. A typical sentence structure is subordinate clause + main clause + -ing clause" (ibidem, 106). This is how he illustrates it:

(a) (subordinate clause) When the piston is drawn sharply upwards,

(b) (main clause) the air below the piston rises,

(c) (-ing clause) thus causing the pressure to fall.

Now compare the following sample sentences:

(7) A negative packing fraction derives from a situation where the isotopic weight is less than the mass number, **inferring** that in the formation of the nucleus from its constituent particles, some mass is converted into energy. (NSE/I/BINDING ENERGY/358)
Ein negativer Packungsanteil leitet sich aus einer Situation her, in der der Massenwert geringer ist als die Massenzahl, **was andeutet,** daß bei der Bildung des Kerns aus seinen Bestandspartikeln ein Teil der Masse in Energie umgewandelt wird.

(8) The rotor may or may not be able to produce its own fan action, depending on the size, speed, and construction of the rotor. (NSE/I/ALTERNATOR/107)

(9) A wide variety of machining operations can be performed on a lathe, requiring appropriate control of the speed of the work spindle and also of the feed... The Norton gear box comprises a tumbler gear which is mounted on a movable lever and can be brought into mesh with any one of a number of other gears, permitting rapid change in the speed of the feed shaft. (HTW/II/LATHE/184)

(10) In a nonliquid system, sulfur dioxide can be absorbed by dry cupric oxide on activated alumina, **thus avoiding the disadvantages of a wet process.**
(NSE/I/ABSORPTION(PROCESS)/7)
In einem nichtflüssigen System kann man Schwefeldioxid durch trockenes Kupfer(II)-oxid auf aktivierter Tonerde absorbieren **und vermeidet so die Nachteile eines Naßverfahrens.**

(11) In this chamber liquid fuel is burned, thereby producing gases with a temperature of about 650°C. (HTW/I/GAS TURBINES/42)

(12) Also, an airfoil of finite thickness provides space for the foundation structure of a lightweight wing, thus removing the structural elements from the drag of the air stream, and thereby reducing the drag. (NSE/I/AIRFOIL/47)

It should be noted that the reduced sentential relative clause may also have a subordinate clause as German equivalent, introduced by **'wobei'**, **'wodurch'**, etc. Thus the Ge version in (10) may be varied as follows:

In einem nichtflüssigen System kann Schwefeldioxid durch trockenes Kupfer(II)-oxid auf aktivierter Tonerde absorbiert werden, **wodurch die Nachteile eines Naßverfahrens vermieden werden.**

If this version is chosen the verb in the subordinate clause must be in the passive unless the alternative construction with the impersonal subject **'man'** is preferred:

"..., wodurch **man** die Nachteile eines Naßverfahrens vermeidet".

#### 2.2.2.6 The Present Participle as Adverbial Clause Equivalent

Basically, there are three participial constructions which, in the interest of conciseness or syntactic compression, are widely used as adverbial clause equivalents in **SE**. These can be distinguished according to whether

(1) the implied subject is identical with that of the main clause,

(2) the participle has its own overt subject that is different from that of the main clause, or

(3) the participle has neither its own subject nor does it provide a link with that of the main clause.

For that reason they are called:

**(1)** the **related** present participle clause,

**(2)** the **absolute** present participle clause, and

**(3)** the **unrelated** present participle clause.

All of them have the function to convey certain semantic relationships which are commonly *causal, circumstantial, conditional, concessive,* or *temporal* in nature.

**(1) The related present participle clause**

This is a many-faceted construction in that it

(1.1) may occur in final, initial, or, less frequently, medial position,

(1.2) may be introduced by a subordinating conjunction, and

(1.3) used as a reduction in verbless adverbial clauses.

(1.1) When the participle is not introduced by a conjunction, there may be some indeterminacy as to the semantic relationship to be inferred. It is therefore important to know that the position of the participle is largely due to the nature of semantic relationship that the writer or speaker wishes the participle to imply. As a rule, participles in final position denote *attendant circumstances* or sometimes also a *causal relationship* (1.1.1), while those in front position usually indicate a *causal* or *conditional* relationship (1.1.2). Furthermore, meanings associated with *tense, aspect* and *mood* can be recovered from the sentential context.

(1.1.1) Since there is no equivalent clause-reducing construction available in Ge, the corresponding alternatives are the devices of **subordination** through the use of subordinating conjunctions, such as **da, weil, indem, wobei, während, wenn, obwohl, so daß,** and **co-ordination** through the use of co-ordinating conjunctions, preferably the conjunction **und**.

(1.1.1.1) **The solvent** containing some dissolved material passes through the porous membrane, **leaving the undissolved residue in the container**.
(NSE/I/EXTRACTION(LIQUID-LIQUID)/1106)
**Das Lösungsmittel**, das einen ungelösten Feststoff enthält, fließt durch ein poröses Membranfilter, **wobei es den ungelösten Rückstand im Behälter zurückläßt**.

(1.1.1.2) In sunlight or magnesium light, **hydrogen combines with chlorine** with violent release of energy, **forming hydrogen chloride** HCL.
(NSE/I/HYDROGEN AS A HEATING FUEL/1495)
Unter Sonnenlicht oder Magnesiumlicht **verbindet sich Wasserstoff** bei gewaltiger Freisetzung von Energie **mit Chlor und bildet Chlorwasserstoff**.

(1.1.1.3) Power diodes made alternators a viable replacement for dc generators, providing improved reliability by eliminating the brushes and commutator.
(NSE/I/ELECTRONICS DEVELOPMENTS RELATED TO AUTOMOTIVE USES/ POWER DEVICES/295)

(1.1.1.4) The reduction process commences with the indirect reduction in the shaft at 400°-700°C, converting part of the ore to iron and part of it to iron monoxide.
(HTW/I/BLAST-FURNACE/332)

(1.1.1.5) ... the design of the combustion chamber should conform to certain principles, namely:

(a) The combustion chamber should be compact, presenting the smallest possible surface area for the loss.
(b) Intensive turbulence of the mixture is essential, so that the ignition spreads rapidly throughout the chamber, leaving no pockets of unburned mixture.
(HTW/II/INCREASING ENGINE EFFICIENCY: MEAN EFFECTIVE PRES-SURE/268)

The present passive participle, used in the following example, is comparatively rare.

(1.1.1.6) When light, x-rays, or other electromagnetic radiation enters a body of matter, it experiences in general two types of attenuation. **Part of it** is subjected to scattering, **being reflected in all directions**, while another portion is absorbed by being converted into other forms of energy. (NSE/I/ABSORPTION COEFFICIENT/6)

Note how cohesion is provided by using a different but semantically related noun phrase, namely "part of it", to refer back to the information "light, x-rays, or other electromagnetic radiation" in the preceding sentence.

(1.1.2) As shown in the following examples, the participle in front position commonly conveys *causal* or *conditional relationships* and thus corresponds to Ge adverbial clauses having the same meanings.

(1.1.2.1) **Rotating at high speed, the impeller** compresses the air by centrifugal action.
(NSE/I/AIRPLANE/AUGMENTATION/66)
**Da sich das Laufrad mit hoher Geschwindigkeit dreht,** komprimiert es die Luft durch die zentrifugale Wirkung.

What has been said concerning the non-availability of an adverbial clause-reducing device in Ge (refer back to (1.1.1)) must be relativized with respect to the front position of the participle. If the participle clause is relatively short, like that in the example above, syntactic one-to-one correspondence with the Ge reduced construction may be admissible. Compare:

**Sich mit hoher Geschwindigkeit drehend** komprimiert das Laufrad die Luft durch die zentrifugale Wirkung.

Occasionally the reduction in Ge is taken further, although at the expense of a change of meaning, by placing the participle in front of the noun that it refers to so that it functions as a noun qualifier:

**Das sich mit hoher Geschwindigkeit drehende Laufrad...**

(1.1.2.2) Acting like lenses, these magnets form the particles into a narrow beam. Depending upon the size and general configuration of a synchrotron, radio-frequency cavities may be variously interspersed among the magnets where the actual acceleration occurs.
(NSE/II/SYNCHROTRONS/2142)

The following two pairs of sentences should also be seen in the light of what has previously been said about cohesion. Notice how the sentences are linked together in order to understand the antecedent of the participle.

(1.1.2.3) Compressors for charging tanks of air used to inflate pneumatic tires at the numerous automotive service stations are of the reciprocating type. Being of small capacity they are generally single acting and air cooled (by exterior fins) since those features are common in small compressors.
(NSE/I/AIR COMPRESSION/RECIPROCATING COMPRESSORS/59)

(1.1.2.4) The various members of the feldspar group show many characteristics in common. Crystallizing in the monoclinic and triclinic systems, they show similarity of crystal habit, cleavage and other physical properties as well as similar chemical relationships.
(NSE/I/FELDSPAR/1120)

(1.1.2.5) Running under no load, such turbines can reach speeds of about 400,000 rpm; under load the speeds are in the range of 200,000 to 300,000 rpm.
(HTW/II/HIGH-SPEED TURBINE DRILL/402)

The participle in front position is particularly common when mathematical equations are to be manipulated. Compare:

(1.1.2.6) Gear trains consisting of more than two gear wheels have the same relationship. In Fig.9, letting the wheels be represented by letters, one has $PR_1R_2R_3 = Wr_1r_2r_3$ and the mechanical advantage is… (NSE/II/MACHINE(SIMPLE)/1743)

(1.1.2.7) Hence, assuming the combined mass of the binary system to be twice that of the sun, and knowing the period of revolution of the system in years, we may find the mean distance between the components of the system in astronomical units.
(NSE/I/DYNAMICAL PARALLAX/947)

The participle in medial position is shown in this sentence:

(1.1.3) As the piston starts to move, carrying the cycle from point A, fuel is injected or sprayed into the cylinder just rapidly enough so that its combustion will keep the pressure up while the volume is being increased, at least up to point B.
(NSE/I/DIESEL ENGINE/878)

(1.2) The participle may be introduced by a subordinating conjunction in which case its adverbial meaning is clearly shown. Compare:

(1.2.1) **The workpiece** is attached to a driven spindle and, **while rotating,** is brought into contact with a cutting tool.
(HTW/II/CUTTING AND MACHINING OF METALS/126)
**Das Werkstück** wird in einer Werkstückspindel eingespannt und wird, **während es sich dreht,** mit einem Schneidwerkzeug in Kontakt gebracht.

(1.2.2) These displacement-type meters, though differing in design and technical features, all operate on the same principle, which will here be described more particularly with reference to the oval-runner meter…
(HTW/II/MEASUREMENT OF FLOW OF FLUIDS/494)

If the participle placed in final position denotes a *temporal relationship*, the use of a conjunction is obligatory in order to prevent misunderstanding. Compare:

(1.2.3) **The system** is expected to save millions of dollars in maintenance hours **while increasing the availability of the craft in flight**.
(NSE/I/AIRCRAFT TYPES/ THE F/A-18 /67)
Es wird erwartet, daß **das System** Millionen an Dollars für Wartungsstunden einspart, **während es die Verfügbarkeit der Maschinen für Flugeinsätze erhöht.**

(1.2.4) Fixed systems require costly retooling when going from one product to the next. (NSE/II/ROBOTS OF THE 1980s/2452)

(1.2.5) ... rapid application of a load, a state of multiaxial stress, and low temperatures all limit slip deformation while encouraging cleavage. (NSE/I/BRITTLE FRACTURE/443)

This type of semantically transparent participial construction, of course, occurs in initial position, too. Compare:

(1.2.6) While gripping the material during its passage through them, the rolls effect a reduction in cross-sectional area, with a corresponding increase in length. (NSE/I/ROLLING/1611)

(1.2.7) Although having a number of limitations, the ammonia maser can be used to describe the principles involved. (NSE/II/MASER/1796)

(1.3) Notice that verbless clauses, which do not have a verb element, but are nevertheless capable of being analyzed into clause elements, can usually be treated as reductions of nonfinite clauses, since it is possible to interpret them as having an omitted present participle, most commonly **being.** Compare:

(1.3.l) CASTING. A process for producing specific shapes of materials by pouring **the material, while in fluid form,** into a shaped cavity (mold) where the material solidifies in the desired shape. (NSE/I/CASTING/520)

The verbless clause introduced by **'while'** can syntactically be made more transparent by inserting **being,** which results in the related participle clause **"...while being in fluid form,...".** Compare also:

(1.3.2) The upper oval element, when in the position shown in Fig.7b, is subjected to a torque of zero magnitude, since the resultant forces acting on each side of the center balance each other. (HTW/II/MEASUREMENT OF FLOW OF FLUIDS/494)

In **SE** this type of covert participial construction is particularly indicative of the relatively frequent use of reduced adjective clauses (cf. section 2.3.3), such as:

(1.3.3) **When cool, the fused powder** forms a slag, which peels off the weld. (HTW/II//FUSION WELDING/136)

**Wenn das geschmolzene pulverförmige Flußmittel kühl ist**, bildet es eine Schlacke, die von der Schweißnaht abblättert.

**(2) The absolute present participle clause**

As stated at the beginning of section 2.2.2.6, this participial construction has its own overt subject and is therefore not explicitly bound to the main or superordinate clause syntactically. As far as its use in general English is concerned Quirk et al. (1985, 1120) point out that "apart from a few stereotyped phrases" (which they exemplify for instance by 'weather/time permitting') "absolute clauses are formal and infrequent." In the special languages of science and technology, however, the absolute participle clause has a well-established and well-founded place among the various clause-reducing devices available. According to Sager et al. (1980, 218) it combines the qualities of clarity and conciseness and makes an important contribution to the economy of expression characteristic of special language communication. It is used to introduce additional descriptive details or other factual information or, in semantic terms, to express a *circumstantial, temporal* or occasionally *causal relationship* between the main and nonfinite clause. That may be the reason for the prevalent final position of this construction in **SE**. In the analysis referred to in section 1.5 only a small number of sentences could be ascertained which show the participle embedded into a complex sentence with the main clause preceding it and either a subordinate or nonfinite clause following it.

The absolute participle clause has no counterpart in Ge where the syntactic alternatives are either an adverbial clause, most commonly introduced by the conjunction **wobei,** or a new sentence, which in this case is to be introduced by the semantically related word **'Dabei'**... Rather than denoting the semantic feature of *simultaneity* which may be indicative of the actions expressed by both the superordinate and nonfinite clause, the absolute participle may also imply the feature of *contrast*, in which case the conjunction **während** is the appropriate word in Ge.

From what has been discussed so far it may be concluded that there is some scope for semantic interpretation, which indeed is true because occasionally there may be some overlapping of semantic relationships. In spite of this potential difficulty the kind of semantic relationship is generally clear from the context.

The following examples illustrate the use of

(2.1) the **present active participle,** including a relatively frequent number of

(2.2) **being + complement,** and the extremely rare construction

(2.3) **there + being,** in which **there** functions as formal subject of **being,** as well as

(2.4) the **present passive participle.**

With regard to the frequency of occurrence of the two participles the assumption appears to be justified that the present passive participle is far more commonly used than its active counterpart.

(2.1) **The use of the present active participle**

(2.1.1) **Silicon** is a semiconductor of electricity, **the conductivity rising** with temperature. (NSE/II/RESEARCH ON SILICON STRUCTURE AND SURFACE PROPERTIES /2581)
**Silizium** ist ein elektrischer Halbleiter, **da die Leitfähigkeit** mit steigender Temperatur **zunimmt.**

(2.1.2) The flanged coupling, one of the simplest types, comprises two halves, each consisting of a flange mounted on the end of a shaft. (HTW/II/COUPLINGS/188)

(2.1.3) Hydrogen molecules dissociate to atoms endothermally at high temperatures (heat of dissociation about 103 cal/gram mole), in an electric arc, or by irradiation. This property is used to effect atomic-hydrogen arc welding, in which hydrogen gas is dissociated by an ac electric arc between two tungsten electrodes, the hydrogen atoms recombining at the metal surface to provide the heat required for welding.
(NSE/I/HYDROGEN/1493)

(2.1.4) When light from the scene being televised is focused onto the surface of the photoconductive layer next to the faceplate, each illuminated element conducts slightly, the current depending upon the amount of light reaching the element.
(NSE/II/TELEVISION/VIDICON/2797)

(2.2) **being + complement**

(2.2.1) An inert atmosphere is required where air must be excluded. **Nitrogen** is one of the three main gases used for such atmospheres, **the other two being carbon monoxide and hydrogen.** (NSE/II/INDUSTRIAL NITROGEN/1982)
Eine Schutzgasatmosphäre ist erforderlich, wo Luft ausgeschlossen werden muß. **Stickstoff** ist eines der drei wichtigsten Gase, das für solche Atmosphären verwendet wird, **während die anderen zwei Kohlenmonoxid und Wasserstoff sind.**

Another possible version in Ge is: **Die anderen zwei sind Kohlenmonoxid und Wasserstoff.**

(2.2.2) When motion can occur about an equilibrium position without disturbing the equilibrium, the system is in neutral (or labile, or indifferent) equilibrium, an example being a marble resting on a perfectly flat plane normal to the direction of gravity. (NSE/I/EQUILIBRIUM/1085)

(2.2.3) The presence of iron and aluminium phosphates also has an effect on total solubility, these compounds being insoluble in water, but soluble in weak acids. (NSE/I/FERTILIZER/PHOSPHOROUS REQUIREMENTS/1129)

(2.2.4) The reasoning behind the fine distinction is that, with cellulose-derived synthetics, one commences with a naturally fibrous material and grossly modifies it, whereas with most other synthetics, the starting materials are strictly chemicals that bear no relationship whatever to a fibrous structure, many of the starting ingredients actually being in the gaseous or liquid phase. (NSE/I/FIBERS/1135)

(2.3) **there + being**

Generally, **the societies** in these countries have not readied themselves to very high energy costs, **there being a realization** that these increased costs will, by and large, come out of so-called discretionary income and, consequently, impact the standard of living in a negative way. (NSE/II/THE ENERGY/ENVIRONMENT CONFLICT/2266)
Im allgemeinen haben sich **die Gesellschaften** in diesen Ländern nicht zu sehr hohen Energiekosten entschlossen, **da sie zu der Erkenntnis gelangt sind,** daß diese erhöhten Kosten im großen und ganzen aus dem sogenannten frei verfügbaren Einkommen zu decken sind und folglich eine negative Auswirkung auf den Lebensstandard haben.

(2.4) **The use of the present passive participle**

(2.4.1) **Vulcanisation** or curing is a chemical reaction whereby the filamentary molecules of rubber are interlinked into a threedimensional network, **this being usually achieved with the aid of sulphur**. (HTW/I/VULCANISATION/356)
**Vulkanisation** ist eine chemische Reaktion, durch die die fadenförmigen Moleküle von Kautschuk zu einer räumlichen Vernetzung verkettet werden, **wobei dies** gewöhnlich **mit Hilfe von Schwefel erreicht wird.**

(2.4.2) The term interferometer may be applied to any arrangement whereby a beam of light from a luminous area clearly defined is separated into two or more parts by partial reflections, the parts being subsequently reunited after traversing different optical paths. (NSE/I/INTERFEROMETER/1579)

(2.4.3) A distinction can be drawn between meteorology, in this sense, and climatology, the latter being primarily concerned with average, not actual, weather conditions. (NSE/II/METEOROLOGY/1834)

(2.4.4) Special forms of the piston pump are the lifting pump, which discharges the liquid when the piston rises; the diaphragm pump, in which a flexible diaphragm takes the place of the piston, this diaphragm being moved to and fro by an actuating rod; ... (HTW/I/PUMPS/20)

(2.5) **'with' + object + present participle**

In this construction, which is a special variant of the absolute present participle clause, the preposition **'with'** is merely used as a function word in order to indicate a particularly close grammatical link between the main and participle clause; **'with'**, so used, has no direct semantic-lexical correspondence in Ge where, as shown above, subordinate adverbial clauses or a new sentence are the corresponding syntactic devices. The preposition **'with' plus object plus participle** constitute a structural unit in which the grammatical **object** is the logical **subject** of the participle. It is used for the purpose of denoting *attendant circumstances* and is therefore preferably placed in final or medial position and less frequently in front position. Considering its position and the choice of translation into Ge, Gerbert (1970, 80) suggests the following conjunctions and prepositional phrases: **da, wenn, infolge, angesichts, bei, ausgehend von.**

Compare:

(2.5.1) However, with increasing load the voltage falls off more rapidly, and above a certain maximum load **the characteristic curve** even **becomes retrograde, with the voltage decreasing** to zero at short-circuit. (HTW/II/DIRECT-CURRENT MACHINES/508)
Jedoch fällt die Spannung bei steigender Belastung schneller ab, und über einer bestimmten Maximalbelastung **wird die Kennlinie** sogar **rückläufig, wobei die Spannung bei Kurzschluß auf null zurückgeht.**

(2.5.2) Extrusion machines are generally hydraulic presses, with capacities ranging from about 500 tons to about 7500 tons. (HTW/II/HOT EXTRUSION OF METALS/124)

(2.5.3) Laminar flow is flow in which the mass of fluid may be considered as advancing in separate laminae (sheets) with simple shear existing at the surface of contact of laminae should there be any difference in mean speed of the separate laminae. (NSE/I/FLUID FLOW/1190)

(2.5.4) With the fast breeder concept offering up to a 100-fold increase in the utilization efficiency of uranium, it appeared to be the logical replacement (second generation) for light water reactors.
(NSE/II/NUCLEAR POWER/FAST BREEDER REACTORS IN PERSPECTIVE/2017)

It is usually possible to recover the present participle **being** in verbless clauses. Compare:

(2.5.5) Fundamentally, **the engine runs quietly** and is comparatively free of vibration, and can be adapted to a rather wide range of fuels, **with torque characteristics suitable for application in vehicles.** (NSE/I/INTERNAL COMBUSTION ENGINE/1581)

The place of the omitted participle is after its logical subject: "with torque characteristics **being** suitable".

Im Grunde genommen **läuft der Motor ruhig** und verhältnismäßig schwingungsfrei, und er kann für ein ziemlich großes Sortiment von flüssigen Kraftstoffen modifiziert werden, **zumal seine Drehmomentkennzahlen** für einen Einsatz in Fahrzeugen **angemessen sind.**

(2.5.6) The drag is also increased giving a steeper gliding angle with flap down than without the use of the flap. (NSE/I/HIGH-LIFT DEVICES/47)

(2.5.7) Combined elements, with the high and intermediate pressure blading in a single casing, offer significant advantages.
(NSE/II/TURBOJET ENGINE/TRENDS IN STEAM TURBINE DESIGN/2878)

**(3) The unrelated present participle clause**

The participle in this nonfinite clause has been described as having neither its own subject nor is the understood subject identifiable with the subject of the main clause. In **SE** this construction is very common where the implied subject is to be identified with the personal pronouns **I, we,** or **you** of the writer(s) or reader(s), or, perhaps more commonly, with the formal **one** to refer to people generally, again including the writer, speaker or reader. In this case the Ge impersonal pronoun **'man'** is the word to match. The participle occurs in initial, medial or final position with the sentential context being usually highly impersonal.

(3.1) Among the participles, which are relatively frequently used in this construction, are **using, assuming, supposing,** and **considering.**

Compare:

(3.1.1) **Using Bohr and Wheeler's calculations, it is found** that the activation energy for fission is 5.2 MeV for uranium-235 and 5.9 MeV for uranium-238.
(NSE/I/BINDING ENERGY/359)
**Wenn man die Berechnungen nach Bohr und Wheeler verwendet, stellt man fest,** daß die Aktivierungsenergie für die Spaltung 5.2 MeV für Uran 235 und 5.9 MeV für Uran 238 beträgt.

(3.1.2) The output voltage, assuming that the open-loop gains $G_1$, $G_2$ $G_3$ and $G_4$ of the separate amplifiers are quite large, is given by... (NSE/I/BRIDGE AMPLIFIER/431)

(3.1.3) Considering a theoretical frictionless system of pulleys, the force (pull) in any part of a continuous rope is constant and equal to P. (NSE/II/MACHINE(SIMPLE)/1743)

(3.1.4) In order to guard against fatigue failures in critical parts such as connecting rods, they should be fabricated from high-quality steels using designs that avoid regions of stress concentrations such as sharp fillets and engraved part numbers. They should be finished overall, avoiding tool or grinding marks. (NSE/I/FATIGUE (METALS)/1114)

The following two examples contrast sharply as to the ease of identifying the antecedents of the unrelated participles. In the first sentence (3.1.5) the participle is preceded by the main clause which expresses an *instruction.* This language function is grammatically signified by the imperative mood of the verb, which enables the reader to interpret the antecedent of the participle as the person spoken to and expected to follow the *instruction.* The second example (3.1.6), by contrast, consists of three sentences, the last showing the participle in front position. The antecedent of this participle is not identifiable unless the reader has understood the information conveyed by the preceding sentences. What might be called '**context awareness**' (cf. also section 2.2.3/(3.1)) is therefore of great help in analysing any kind of clause-reducing devices.

(3.1.5) Determine the size and shape required for the furnace, giving consideration to location, the space requirements of burners or fuel bed, and incorporating sufficient furnace volume to accomplish complete combustion. (NSE/I/BOILER DESIGN/398)

(3.1.6) If the true values of the high order interactions are zero, their estimates will provide estimates of experimental error. An experiment with many factors can then be carried out in a single replication, a suitable estimate of error still being available. Extending this notion, it is possible to carry out an experiment using only a suitably chosen fraction 1/g of all the possible treatment combinations.
(NSE/I/FACTORIAL EXPERIMENT/1110)

(3.2) Like the related present participle the unrelated present participle can be introduced by subordinating conjunctions. Compare:

(3.2.1) **The negatives are developed,** printed on metal and etched in much the same way as **when making a monochrome half tone plate.** (HTW/I/COLOUR PRINTING/292)
**Die Negative werden genauso entwickelt,** auf eine Metallplatte gedruckt und geätzt, als **wenn man eine einfarbige Halbtonplatte herstellt.**

Note that from a stylistic point of view a nominal translation is preferable: "...wie bei der Herstellung einer einfarbigen Halbtonplatte".

(3.2.2) The large size of present water reactors and the nuclear effects which can occur, such as xenon redistribution, stuck rods, and reactivity anomalies requires that emphasis be placed on instrumentation and control systems if high plant availability is to be maintained, while providing the necessary protection due to abnormal occurrences. (NSE/II/NUCLEAR POWER/INSTRUMENTATION/2006)

(3.2.3) A very small reverse current flows, sustained only by the thermally generated minority carriers of both zones which are swept across the junction. When applying a very high potential (e.g., 1,000 volts), these highly accelerated carriers generate more carriers by avalanche multiplication due to impact with lattice.
(NSE/II/RECTIFIERS/SEMICONDUCTOR RECTIFIERS/2410)

(3.2.4) It is possible when using alternating current to cause current to flow by inductive coupling as well as by direct contact between electrode and electrolyte.
(NSE/I/MEASUREMENT FUNDAMENTALS/1030)

### 2.2.3 Perfect Participle Constructions

Compared to the frequent and versatile use of the present and past participles, the perfect participle plays a minor role in **SE**. It usually denotes an action that is complete or that happened before the next action starts. As a clause-reducing device it can only function as an adverbial clause equivalent, whereas its use as a complement was previously indicated in section 2.2.2.4. Like the other participles it may be used as

**(1)** a **related** perfect participle clause,

**(2)** an **absolute** perfect participle clause, and

**(3)** an **unrelated** perfect participle clause.

**(1) The related perfect participle clause**

(1.1) **The use of the perfect participle active**

(1.1.1) In its many decades of use, **the open-hearth process became a mature technology having benefited from** numerous **technical improvements.**
(NSE/I/HISTORICAL OPEN-HEARTH PROCESS/1607)
In den vielen Jahrzehnten seiner Anwendung **wurde das Siemens-Martin-Verfahren eine ausgereifte Technologie, nachdem es von** zahlreichen **technischen Verbesserungen profitiert hatte.**

(1.1.2) The solids settle to the screen surface and form a filter bed through which the liquid passes. The liquid continues through the basket and is discharged from the machine, while the solids, having formed a uniform filter-bed thickness in the cylinder basket, are assisted to discharge by a pusher ram. (NSE/I/CENTRIFUGING/552)

This sample sentence shows the participle immediately after its antecedent "the solids" in a position which is typically occupied by the postmodifying (relative-clause reducing) participle and thus may pose some difficulty for analysis if the semantic role of the perfect participle, namely to express *anteriority,* is unknown or disregarded. The adverbial nature of the perfect participle is quite evident since a temporal sequence of events can be inferred whenever it is used in this construction.

(1.1.3) The standing waves in the cavity act on the electrons and cause them to change speed so that they arrive at the second cavity (catcher) in bunches, having passed out of the first into a field-free space and then into the second through the grids in the sides of the cavities. (NSE/II/MICROWAVE TUBES/1854)

(1.2) **The use of the perfect participle passive**

(1.2.1) **Two streams of vapor are removed** from a point near the axis of the centrifuge, **having been separated by diffusion** through the centrifugal field.
(NSE/I/CENTRIFUGING/553)
**Zwei Dampfströme werden** von einem Punkt nahe der Zentrifugenachse **entfernt, nachdem sie durch Diffusion** durch das Zentrifugalfeld **getrennt worden sind.**

(1.2.2) Although still widely in use, coaxial cable is no longer favored in specifications for new broadband communications systems, having been replaced in preference by microwave radio and optical fiber systems. (NSE/II/LOCAL TELEPHONE LOOP/2778)

(1.2.3) When compared to the other electrical quantities, the *v a r* is a relatively new term, having been recognized by international agreement in 1930.
(NSE/I/ELECTRIC POWER AND ENERGY MEASUREMENT / POWER FACTOR /1112)

**(2) The absolute perfect participle clause**

If the turbine were blocked stationary and had its gates opened, the water would issue from the turbine as from a nozzle. Now, by removing the blocking, let these nozzles begin to rotate, and **the absolute velocity of water** leaving them **is found to be diminishing, the energy having been absorbed by the runner.**
(NSE/I/HYDRAULIC TURBINES/1468)

**(3) The unrelated perfect participle clause**

(3.1) **Having determined the path** which the space vehicle is to follow, **the next step is to determine the guidance** necessary to keep it on that path.
(NSE/II/SPACE VEHICLE GUIDANCE AND CONTPOL/2651)

A paraphrase by the corresponding finite clause reveals that the subject of the subordinate clause is either I, **we** or perhaps **one.**

**After one has/ I /we/ have determined the path...**

Since the sentential context does not contain any clues to one of these options, the preceding macrocontext had to be scanned in order to locate the antecedent that corresponds to the implicit subject of the participle clause "**Having determined the path** ... ". After scanning four (!) sentences the antecedent of the participle could be identified in the clause "**We** can calculate the path ... ". Operations like this are often necessary for a correct translation of the unrelated participle into Ge. Compare:

**Nachdem wir die Bahn bestimmt haben,** der das Raumfahrzeug folgen soll, besteht der nächste Schritt darin, die Führung zu bestimmen, die notwendig ist, um es auf dieser Bahn zu halten.

(3.2) As reported by the investigators, once having determined the distance to each galaxy, Hubble's law is applied to ascertain how fast the galaxy should be receding from Earth as the result of cosmic expansion. (NSE/I/MOTION OF GALAXIES/1271)

#### 2.2.4 Past Participle Constructions

##### 2.2.4.1 Premodification of a noun

As a simple attributive the past participle shares with the present active participle some adjectival characteristics in that it may be modified by an adverb or adverbial phrase, for instance.

(1) A **severely cold-worked metal** may easily have a dislocation density $10^6$ times greater than in the same **unworked metal**. (NSE/I/ANNEALING/167)
Ein **extrem kaltumgeformter metallischer Werkstoff** kann leicht eine Versetzungsdichte aufweisen, die $10^6$ mal größer als diejenige des gleichen **nicht umgeformten metallischen Werkstoffes ist.**

(2) These abnormally absorbed frequencies constitute, collectively, the "absorption spectrum" of the medium, and appear as dark lines or bands in the otherwise continuous spectrum of the transmitted light. (NSE/I/ABSORPTION SPECTRUM/7)

(3) By heating for a controlled time at slightly elevated temperatures, even further strengthening is possible and the properties are stabilized.
(NSE/I/ALUMINIUM ALLOYS/HEAT-TREATABLE ALLOYS/115)

(4) The magnitude of the effect of accelerated flight is well illustrated by considering the centrifugal force on an airplane following a curved flight path in the vertical plane.
(NSE/I/ACCELERATED FLIGHT (AIRPLANE)/9)

Needless to say that the past participle occurs most frequently as an adjective in **SE**. Take, for instance, "elevated temperatures" and "curved flight path" which can be semantically related to "higher temperatures" and "curvy flight path" respectively. The adjectival nature of the past participle is obvious in the following two sentences:

(5) Correct processing involves heating the plastic sufficiently for it to flow freely (not forcing **half-melted plastic** through a die or into a mold) and cooling it slowly.
(NSE/I/CELLULOSE/PROCESSING/548)

(6) Upon emerging from the washing tanks, the film is squeegeed to remove surplus water and then conducted through a series of rollers into a **temperature-and-humidity-controlled drying cabinet**.
(NSE/II/PHOTOGRAPHY AND IMAGERY/PROCESSING/2210)

The two noun qualifiers "half-melted" and "temperature-and-humidity-controlled" are clearly adjective compounds. As there are no paradigmatic tensed forms based on *to half-melt or *to temperature-control, the two attributives cannot be related to verbs.

#### 2.2.4.2 Postmodification of a Noun

Unlike the past participle used as a premodifier, the past participle when used as a postmodifier is verbal in nature. In general English some unmodified or unexpanded past participles in fixed expressions are said to have postposition (cf. Quirk et al. 1985, 1329), e.g.

the amount **demanded/asked** for services **rendered**

the earliest inventions **known**

Prepositional verbs normally follow the noun, too:

the pages **referred to**

the sum **agreed upon**

In **SE**, by contrast, postmodification of a noun by means of an unmodified past participle is not uncommon. Swale's assumption that "it seems that the past participle only follows the nominal when it refers back to something already explained more fully in previous sentences" (1971, 139) can be substantiated by many examples, such as:

(1) The potential difference across an inductor is directly proportional to the rate of change of the **magnetic flux intercepted by the coil.** Conversely, **the flux intercepted** may be expressed as the time integral of the potential difference.
(NSE/I/AMPLIFIER CONFIGURATIONS/141)
Der Potentialunterschied an einem Leiter ist direkt proportional zur Geschwindigkeit der Veränderung **des Magnetflusses, der von der Spule aufgefangen wird.** Umgekehrt kann **der aufgefangene Magnetfluß (or: der Magnetfluß, der aufgefangen wird....)** als das Zeitintegral des Potentialunterschiedes ausgedrückt werden.

(2) A relatively new process may reduce the electrical energy requirements by as much as 30%... Reports from Alcoa indicate that the 30% less electricity required (as compared with the most efficient Hall process) previously expected has been substantiated.
(NSE/I/ALUMINIUM/NEW PROCESSES/110)

(3) Under the conditions considered, the magnetic field strength above the electron path is thereby intensified, and the field strength below it is reduced.
(HTW/I/ELECTRODYNAMICS/58)

More examples of common past participles used in postposition include:

| | |
|---|---|
| the process **involved** (i.e. 'in question') | a field such as the one **described** |
| the alloy **concerned** (i.e. 'in question') | the equipment **used** |
| the great majority of glass **produced** | the hydrogen **applied** |

Notice, however, that the past participle can occur in postposition without necessarily referring back to something discussed or explained in previous sentences. Compare:

(4) Upon ignition of this fuel, the heat developed raises the pressure of the products of combustion, or, at least, maintains the pressure during some motion of the piston. (NSE/I/INTERNAL COMBUSTION ENGINE/ 1581)

(5) Let it be assumed that an object at rest or in a state of uniform motion receives a disturbing force. Depending on the kind of stability possessed, it might react with one of the motions shown in the accompanying figure. (NSE/II/STABILITY(MECHANICAL)/2685)

(6) Where only two principal materials are involved, binary alloy is the term used. (NSE/I/ALLOYS/98)

(7) Such a charge-dominated collection of ionized matter is known as plasma. This plasma at such extremely high temperatures cannot be confined by walls made of materials, known or imagined. (NSE/I/FUSION POWER/1263)

Note also that the past participle comes after the noun in the reduction with **'so'** and **'thus'**, e.g.:

(8) Although the compression **thus achieved** is of limited magnitude, staging the compression in a series of nozzles, with intermediate coolers for partial condensation of vapor, allows moderate compression ratios to be achieved. (NSE/I/AXIAL-FLOW COMPRESSORS/61)

As this example shows, backward reference to the information given just before can be made explicit by using **thus** in front of the participle.

#### 2.2.4.3 Inversion in Declarative Sentences

Like the present participle, discussed in section 2.2.2.3, the past participle frequently occurs in initial position as inverted predicate used with the connective **be.** Compare:

(1) **Mounted on the shaft,** which is driven in the clockwise direction by a spring or a weight, **is the so-called escape wheel,** which is in fact a ratchet wheel. (HTW/II/LOCKING AND ARRESTING MECHANISMS/216)
**Auf der Welle,** die durch eine Feder oder ein Gewicht im Uhrzeigersinn gedreht wird, **befindet sich das sogenannte Hemmungsrad,** das eigentlich ein Sperrad ist.

(2) Then, subtracted from this figure is the observed recession velocity as determined from the galaxy's red shift. (NSE/I/MOTIONS OF GALAXIES/1271)

(3) As a result, voltages corresponding to the signals R and L respectively are produced in the resistors of these branches. Superimposed on both these signals is still a 38 kHz oscillation, but this is suppressed in the following resistance-capacitance sections. (HTW/II/VHF STEREOPHONIC BROADCASTING/538)

Apart from **subtracted** and **superimposed,** used in the examples (2) and (3), Gerbert's list of past participles commonly encountered at the head of inverted predicates (1970, 61) - **shown, pictured, installed, interposed, incorporated, accommodated, mounted, bolted, built, connected, attached, hinged** - might be extended by the addition of **associated, related, located, fitted** and **used.**

Notice that *state* rather than *process* can be expressed unambiguously by inversion of predicate and subject with the past participle placed in initial position.

**2.2.4.4 The Past Participle as Complement of a Clause Element**

**(1) The past participle as predicative subject complement**

This construction seems to be less common than its counterpart with the present participle, dealt with in section 2.2.2.4. The examples given below show it after verbs of *judgement/opinion* and *perception* as well as after *durative* **keep** and **hold.** Compare:

(1.1) **The thin boundary layer might be imagined subdivided into a great many lamina of air** parallel to the surface and extending out to the limits of the boundary layer. (NSE/I/AERODYNAMICS AND AEROSTATICS/EFFECTS OF VISCOSITY/45)
**Man könnte sich die dünne Grenzschicht als in viele Luftschichten unterteilt vorstellen,** die parallel zur Oberfläche verlaufen und sich bis zu den Rändern der Grenzschicht erstrecken.

(1.2) For the time being, the masses of all substances present will be supposed fixed, and to achieve simplicity it will be given that there are no substances present whose properties depend on their previous histories; ... (NSE/II/THERMODYNAMICS/2810)

(1.3) The kinetic theory assumes that the velocity of a molecule may depend on the conditions in the region where it has just suffered a collision, but is otherwise random - in other words, independent of its previous history. This assumption permits one to use the methods of probability theory even though, in classical mechanics, the actual motions of the molecules are regarded as completely determined by their initial configurations. (NSE/II/KINETIC THEORY/IRREVERSIBILITY/1657)

(1.4) Weather satellites, communications satellites and probes have one feature in common: they are unmanned. They are put into orbit or space trajectory by means of launching rockets, and their electronic equipment is powered by solar batteries - i.e., **storage batteries** which **are kept charged by current** generated in solar cells. (HTW/II/SATELLITES AND SPACE PROBES/386)

Wettersatelliten, Nachrichtensatelliten und Raumsonden haben ein gemeinsames Merkmal - sie sind unbemannt. Sie werden mit Hilfe von Trägerraketen in die Umlaufbahn oder Raumflugbahn gebracht, und ihre elektronischen Geräte werden mit Energie aus Sonnenbattetien betrieben, d.h. **Akkumulatoren, die ständig geladen sind durch elektrischen Strom**, der in Solarzellen erzeugt wird.

(1.5) Projecting into the glass tube is one end of a metal rod that is held gripped in the middle. (HTW/I/RESONANCE/ECHO/184)

(1.6) In a modern aircraft the equipment usually takes the form of an automatic direction finder (radio compass) whose antenna is kept directed at a particular radio beacon by means of an electrical sensing circuit. (HTW/I/AIR NAVIGATION/572)

**(2) The past participle as predicative object complement**

In **SE** this construction is common after a number of verbs which include **have,** denoting a *resulting state, causative* **have, make** and **get,** *durative* **keep,** and, less frequently, verbs of *judgement/opinion* and *perception* (cf. also section 2.4.2). Sager/Dungworth (1980, 1084) relate it to the passive and state: "The construction **have + obj. + past participle** can be used as a substitute for the passive. It is employed where the tense character of the passive is considered inappropriate, e.g.

A motor **has its primary winding connected to**...

instead of

The primary winding of a motor is connected to...

Certain alloys **have their properties modified by...**

instead of

The properties of certain alloys are modified by...

These constructions are then interpreted as describing a *state* rather than a *process*, a distinction made in German by the use of **'sein'** + past participle, e.g.

Die Eigenschaften gewisser Legierungen **sind... verändert**.

Die Eigenschaften gewisser Legierungen **werden ... verändert**."

The aforementioned semantic classes of verbs taking the past participle as object complement are illustrated by the following sample sentences:

(2.1) **The series generator has the field winding connected in series** with the armature winding.
(HTW/II/DIRECT-CURRENT MACHINES/508)
**Beim Reihenschlußgenerator ist die Feldwicklung** mit der Ankerwicklung **in Reihe geschlossen.**

(2.2) Spur gears are those which have their teeth cut parallell to parallel axes of rotation.
(NSE/II/MACHINE(SIMPLE)/1743)

(2.3) A solid brick wall of more than one layer thickness has the different layers of brick bonded into each other by the use of headers, that is, brick laid perpendicular to the face of the wall. (NSE/I/BRICKWORK/431)

(2.4) It so happens that the acoustic pressure of the sound emitted by motor vehicles is relatively low in this same frequency range of 2000-5000 cycles/secs. It is therefore advantageous to ensure that the frequencies of the sounds made by a motor horn are within this range: **the horn will** thus better **be able to make itself heard** above the general noise of the traffic. (HTW/I/ELECTRIC HORN/518)

(2.5) **The pressure** exerted by the gland (screwed or bolted on) **keeps the packing tightly pressed** against the valve stem. (HTW/I/VALVES, COCKS AND TAPS/230)
**Der Druck,** der von der Stopfbuchsenbrille (die aufgeschraubt oder verbolzt ist) ausgeübt wird, **drückt die Dichtung eng an den Ventilschaft.**

(2.6) If we have enough of these streamtubes, all of the same width, but whose heights may vary as velocity varies, **we might imagine them stacked,** one on another, as shown in Fig.1, and be thus encompassing the whole flow of air through a given system.
(NSE/I/AERODYNAMICS AND AEROSTATICS/STREAMTUBE/45)

#### 2.2.4.5 The Past Participle as Relative Clause Equivalent

Whereas the **present participle,** when used in this function, appears at the head of a reduced **active** relative clause, the **past participle** appears at the head of a reduced **passive** relative clause. The antecedent is always identical with the implied subject of the postmodifying participle clause, as it is with the present participle construction.

The reduced participle clause results from deleting both the **relative pronoun** and the **auxiliary.**

Compare:

The engine **(that is/was) repaired** by that mechanic ...

The past participle clause will be interpreted, according to context, as equivalent to the finite clause in the present or past tense. Thus:

The engine **repaired** by that mechanic **is** in poor condition.
Der Motor, **der** von dem Kfz-Schlosser **repariert wird, ist** in einem schlechten Zustand.
The engine **repaired** by that mechanic **before he left ...**
Der Motor, **der** von dem Kfz-Schlosser **repariert wurde, bevor er wegging...**

The relatively frequent occurrence of reduced passive relative clauses in **SE** is due to the writer's (or speaker's) desire for objectivity and conciseness of expression, "especially when a sequence of relative clauses occurs and reduction eliminates the need for repetition of the relative pronoun" (Sager et al. 1980, 223). Compare:

(1) Propeller efficiency is expressed as the ratio of **thrust power delivered to engine power required to turn the propeller.** (NSE/I/PROPELLER/63)
Der Propellerwirkungsgrad wird als Quotient der **Schubkraft** ausgedrückt, **die der Triebwerksleistung zugeführt wird, welche erforderlich ist, um den Propeller zu drehen.**

(2) However, in speaking of air preheaters, what is ordinarily meant is the heater employed for raising the temperature of air used for combustion of a fuel.
(NSE/I/AIR PREHEATER/77)

(3) The functioning principle of an ordinary thermometer is based on the property of thermal expansion possessed by most substances, i.e., they expand when heated and contract on cooling. (HTW/I/TEMPERATURE MEASURING INSTRUMENTS/12)

Notice that a past participle does not necessarily require a passive translation into Ge. Depending on the semantic nature of the antecedent, e.g. in the last sentence (3) "the property of thermal expansion" = Ge "die Eigenschaft der thermischen Ausdehnung", the past participle clause "possessed by most substances" requires an **active** version in Ge, namely "die die meisten Stoffe **aufweisen".**

(4) A rotating impeller mounted in a casing and revolved at high speed will cause a fluid which is continuously admitted near the center of rotation to experience an outward flow and a pressure rise due to centrifugal action.
(NSE/I/CENTRIFUGAL COMPRESSORS/60)

#### 2.2.4.6 The Past Participle as Adverbial Clause Equivalent

What has been stated in section 2.2.2.6 concerning the types of present participle constructions and the semantic relationships expressed by them when they are used as adverbial clause equivalents, applies equally well to the past participle constructions which will be discussed in this section. Thus the types of past participle clauses to be distinguished are:

(1) the **related** past participle clause, whose subject is identical with that of the main clause,

(2) the **absolute** past participle clause, which has its own overt subject that is different from that of the main clause, and

(3) the **unrelated** past participle clause, which has neither its own subject nor does it provide a link with that of the main clause.

**(1) The related past participle clause**

(1.1) The ascertained sample sentences representing this type of nonfinite clause show the past participle almost always in initial position, which confirms Gerbert's view (1970, 77) that such nonfinite clauses allow the specialist writer to distinguish between attributes of the subject which differ in their relative importance: characteristics such as materials, properties, design and processing features can be referred to initially and more important details dealt with later in the sentence. Past participle clauses in this position are most commonly *causal, conditional, circumstantial* or *temporal* in meaning. In Ge either adverbial clauses introduced by subordinating conjunctions or participle clauses are the corresponding structures. Compare:

(1.1.1) **Made of ablative material, the shield** dissipates heat by melting and vaporizing. (HTW/II/REENTRY AND ABLATION/370)

It is usually possible to see a correspondence with a finite clause with a form of **'be'** and a **pronoun subject** having the same reference as a noun or pronoun in the same sentence. For example in sentence (1.1.1) the following insertions might be made:

> **(Since/Because/As it is) made of ablative material, the shield** dissipates heat by melting and vaporizing.

This sentence is structurally equivalent to the Ge version:

**Da der Schutzschild aus Ablationswerkstoff hergestellt ist**, dissipiert er die Wärme durch Schmelzen und Verdampfen.

(1.1.2) **Invented** over three centuries ago, **the liquid-in-glass thermometer reached its zenith** as a temperature measuring device in the early 1800s.
(NSE/II/LIQUID-IN-GLASS THERMOMETER/1720)
**Nachdem das Glasthermometer vor mehr als dreihundert Jahren erfunden worden war, erreichte es seinen Zenit** als Temperaturmeßgerät Anfang des neunzehnten Jahrhunderts.

Consider the alternative version in Ge:

**Vor über dreihundert Jahren erfunden, erreichte das Glasthermometer seinen Zenit** als Temperaturmeßgerät Anfang des neunzehnten Jahrhunderts.

(1.1.3) Composed of 18 microscopically thin coated layers in a rectangular format for both horizontal and vertical composition, this film is able to produce photographs of improved color separation, saturation and brilliance.
(NSE/II/PHOTOGRAPHY AND IMAGERY/DIRECT POSITIVE IMAGES/2203)

(1.1.4) Mounted on a milling machine, the cutter takes successive cuts from the gear blank, which is rotated the correct distance after each cut to give the desired spacing of the teeth.
(HTW/II/GEAR CUTTING/166)

(1.1.5) A different arrangement is shown in Fig.2, in which the injection nozzle is located outside the cylinder, protected from high pressure and temperature.
(HTW/II/FUEL INJECTION AND SUPERCHARGING/278)

(1.2) As in clauses with a related present participle, frequent use is made of subordinating conjunctions in related past participle clauses, some of which may occur in initial, medial and final position within a sentence. Notice that participles expressing a *causal* relationship are usually used without a conjunction, whereas the use of some conjunctions is obligatory, e.g. **although, though, as if/as though, unless, if, once**, and in final position **when and while.** Some conjunctions are most common, e.g. **when** and **as,** whereas others, such as **until, once,** and **while** are apparently less common.

These clauses can be easily related to finite clauses containing both the **subject** and the appropriate form of '**be**'. Compare:

(1.2.1) Metals such as lead and tin are malleable at ordinary temperatures, **whereas others,** such as iron, **become malleable only when heated.** (HTW/II/FORGING/118)

**When they are heated...**

Metallische Werkstoffe, wie z. B. Blei und Zinn, sind bei gewöhnlichen Temperaturen schmiedbar, **während andere,** zum Beispiel Eisen, **nur schmiedbar werden, wenn sie erwärmt werden.**

(1.2.2) These materials are ferroelectric and, when prepolarized, exhibit piezoelectric behavior. (NSE/I/REVERSIBLE TRANSDUCERS/24)

(1.2.3) When thus energised, this last-mentioned relay interrupts a flow of current to the actuating electromagnet of a valve... (HTW/I/RAILWAY SAFETY DEVICES/532)

(1.2.4) Modern chromatography plays three major roles in science and industry, separately or in combination: (1) As a means for identifying and quantifying the ingredients of a mixture of chemical substances - as used in the laboratory for quality control, for example,...
(NSE/I/CHROMATOGRAPHY/625)

This type of reduced adverbial clause must not be mixed up with what Swales (1971, 153) describes as a **linking 'as' clause** which refers to the whole main clause and therefore has no subject. It is employed with verbs which allow it to be used as an ideal means of back and forward reference, i.e. it functions like a thought-connective. Compare:

**As stated** at the beginning of this section...

As has been stated...

**As shown** in Fig.1...

As is shown...

**As demonstrated** in the following experiment...

As will be demonstrated...

Nevertheless, since verbs of *statement, description, judgement/opinion* and *perception* are involved in the use of subjectless **linking 'as' clauses,** it is usually possible to interpret the implied subject of the past participle as being the writer or speaker or, ultimately, any other person whose opinions, thoughts, etc. are referred to.

(1.2.5) The internal combustion engine is of a type tending to deliver its power cyclically, and in a fashion which would be very fluctuating unless balanced by the use of a heavy flywheel, or by overlapping of power impulses through multicylindered arrangements.

...All of these factors, while not fully idealized, have benefited from tremendous investments in research over the past decade or two. Although invented much earlier, the Sterling engine was manufactured in the Netherlands during the World War II era as a power plant for portable generators.
(NSE/I/INTERNAL COMBUSTION ENGINE/1581)

(1.2.6) Once filled, the mold is moved to an oven for cure.
(NSE/I/CELLULOSE/PROCESSING/548)

(1.2.7) Small compressors may be operated with high compression ratios (8-12) if desired because cooling is more effective in small cylinders and mechanical strength is readily provided. (NSE/I/RECIPROCATING COMPRESSORS/60)

(1.2.8) In a cartesian coordinate system, the location of the center for the coordinate system is the center of the junction of the first two joints. Except for literally moving the robot to another factory location, this center does not move. In effect, it is tied to the "world" as if anchored in concrete.
(NSE/II/CLASSIFICATION OF ROBOTS/AXES OF MOTION/2453)

**(2) The absolute past participle clause**

(2.1) This participial construction has been described as having its own overt subject that is different from that of the main clause. In **SE** it is much less common than the absolute present participle clause, which is in fact well established as an appropriate clause-reducing device. My researches into the use of the absolute past participle resulted in just four sentences, which show the participle clause in final position. As shown in section 2.2.2.6, the absolute participle construction corresponds to an adverbial finite clause in Ge. Depending on the length or complexity of the sentence, the participle clause may also correspond to a new sentence in Ge. Compare:

(2.1.1) **Billions of miles of experience with the DC-10s provided much needed experience** to design the new cockpit and system, **this experience utilized by a design team** made up of pilots, flight engineers, and human factor specialists.
(NSE/I/AIRPLANE/ AUTOMATICITY AND COMPUTERIZATION/71)
**Millliarden von Flugmeilen mit den DC-10-Maschinen lieferten die dringend benötigten Erfahrungen,** um das neue Cockpit und Computersystem zu konstruieren, **wobei diese Erfahrungen von einem Konstruktionsteam aus Piloten, Bordingenieuren und Spezialisten für Arbeitspsychologie verwertet wurden.**

..., **und diese Erfahrungen wurden...** verwertet.
**Dabei wurden diese Erfahrungen...** verwertet.

(2.1.2) The carrier currents which were routed to the carrier circuits by the first high-pass filter are then routed to their respective channels for demodulating by band-pass filters, each designed to pass one channel. (NSE/I/FILTER(COMMUNICATIONS SYSTEM)/1145)

(2.1.3) Thus, early designers developed a clever, innovative "teach-and-playback" methodology for robot programming. In the teach mode, the robot is directed through various movements in sequence, this accomplished by actually manually guiding the robot through its complete act so to speak. (NSE/II/PROGRAMMING ROBOTS/2456)

(2.1.4) In addition to thermal and mechanical efficiency, the boiler designer must consider the impact of environment controls and the purpose for which the steam is generated - for powering turbines in the production of electricity, for processing use, as in a chemical plant (steam heat, reactions, etc.), or for the combined objectives of power production and process use, the latter frequently referred to as c o g e n e r a t i o n. (NSE/I/BOILER/393)

(2.2) **'with' + object + past participle**

Like the active present participle construction introduced by **'with'** (refer back to section 2.2.2.6/(2.5)), the passive past participle construction is a special variant of the **absolute participle** clause, with the preposition **'with'** being merely a function word used to indicate a particularly close grammatical link between the main and participle clause. It is usually used in final or initial position and, amazingly, seems to be given preference over the normal absolute past participle clause discussed in the previous section (2.1). The semantic relationships expressed by the participle are most commonly *circumstantial, temporal* or *causal* in nature. Since in Ge the device of subordination is generally used, these meanings become explicit by choosing semantically adequate conjunctions to introduce the respective adverbial finite clauses, although a participle clause may occasionally be preferred in Ge, too. Compare:

(2.2.1) But, **with many thousands of robots installed, their presence is** indeed **impressive**. (NSE/II/ROBOTS IN PERSPECTIVE/2452)

Aber **nachdem jetzt viele Tausende von Robotern eingesetzt worden sind, ist ihre Präsenz** in der Tat **beeindruckend**.

Aber bei den vielen Tausenden von eingesetzten Robotern ist ihre Präsenz in der Tat beeindruckend.

(2.2.2) With the throttle closed, only a small amount of air can flow through the induction pipe and is unable to carry along any petrol from the choke tube. (HTW/I/CARBURETTOR/478)

(2.2.3) A typical example of a giant multistage rocket is the Saturn 5, which took America's first astronauts to the moon. ... The first stage was of very heavy and powerful construction, with five Fl motors powered by kerosene and liquid air, developing a thrust of 7.5 million pounds. (HTW/II/MULTISTAGE ROCKETS/368)

(2.2.4) The concept for constructing a STEM dates back to 1963, growing out of the techniques and practices of research in nuclear and high-energy physics, with minimal consideration given to the large record of experience gained with the STEM. (NSE/I/HIGH-RESOLUTION SCANNING TRANSMISSION ELECTRON MICROSCOPE (STEM)/1044)

(2.2.5) Basically, the turboprop engine is a turbojet with most of the heat converted to the shaft power by the turbine wheels, leaving very little for jet reaction. ... All of the control requirements of the turbojet are present in the turboprop engine with additional requirement imposed by the propeller. (NSE/I/TURBOPROP ENGINES/66)

In verbless clauses introduced by **'with'** the omitted past participle can be recovered by a thorough analysis of the sentential context. Compare:

(2.2.6) The temperature and flow rate of the metal, the mold temperature, the flow rate of the cooling water and the speed of descent of the billet must all be accurately interadjusted. **With several molds side by side, the installation can be designed** to produce a number of billets simultaneously. (HTW/II/CONTINUOUS CASTING/98)
**With several molds used side by side, ...**
**Wenn mehrere Kokillen nebeneinander verwendet werden,...**

(2.2.7) In the older type of power station with reciprocating steam engines, the rotor of the generator is generally constructed as a flywheel with the magnetic pole windings round its rim. (HTW/I/ELECTRIC GENERATOR (DYNAMO)/60)

**(3) The unrelated past participle clause**

(3.1) In **SE** this construction is very rare as compared to the use of the unrelated present participle clause, with which it shares the characteristics of neither having a subject nor a syntactic link with the subject of the main clause. The implied subject, however, is usually **it,** while in Ge the impersonal pronoun **'man'** is preferred. Compare:

(3.1.1) In recent years, lightning has been found to be much more complex and variable **than previously believed.** (NSE/II/ LIGHTNING/1706)
In den letzten Jahren hat man festgestellt, daß Blitze viel komplexer und variabeler sind, **als man vorher geglaubt hatte.**

(3.1.2) **Viewed as a whole,** the working of a modern mine comprises a large number of interlinked operations which require careful advance planning, with adequate allowance for compensation and latitude of critical points in the system.
(HTW/II/MINES AND MINING/66)

(3.2) The following two examples show the unrelated past participle clause as a nonfinite clause that is introduced by a conjunction. Notice that the participle has its antecedent in the preceding sentence where it functions as the subject of the main clause. Compare:

(3.2.1) **Steels** containing less than 0.83% carbon are known as hypoeutectoid steels. **When cooled slowly, the microstructure of these steels** consists of pearlite and ferrite.
(NSE/I/EFFECT OF INGREDIENTS ON STEEL/1614)
**Stähle,** die weniger als 0.83% Kohlenstoff enthalten, sind als untereutektoide Stähle **bekannt. Wenn sie langsam abgekühlt werden,** besteht **das Mikrogefüge dieser Stähle** aus Perlit und Ferrit.

(3.2.2) Steels containing more than 0.83% carbon are known as hypereutectoid steels. When cooled slowly, their microstructure is comprised of pearlite and cementite.
(NSE/I/EFFECT OF INGREDIENTS ON STEEL/1614)

**2.2.5 The Multiple Use of Participles**

In the preceding sections the participles have been described in terms of their structures, functions and versatile uses. Moreover, they have been shown to be conspicuous by their high frequency of occurrence. This section will demonstrate that a single sentence or even successive sentences may have an extremely complex structure due to the use of a large number of participial constructions. The following sample sentences are therefore given to exemplify

**(1)** the versatile use of participles in a sentence as well as in successive sentences,

**(2)** the use of coordinate participles in a sentence: of the same type (2.1) as well as of active and passive constructions (2.2); finally,

**(3)** the repeated use of the same structures in succession.

**(1) The versatility of participles both in a sentence and in successive sentences**

(1.1) Let us stick to the simple broad picture **showing** all matter as **made up** of atoms **each having** at the centre an electrically positive "sun" or nucleus, **with electrically negative electrons circulating** around it like planets, **the number of such electrons depending**

**on** the element **concerned** (extracted from: Baakes 1967, 16).

Bleiben wir bei dem einfachen allgemeinen Bild, das uns die gesamte Materie aus Atomen **zusammengesetzt zeigt,** von denen **jedes** im Zentrum eine elektrisch positive "Sonne" oder einen Kern **hat, während elektrisch negative Elektronen** diesen so wie Planeten die Sonne **umkreisen, wobei die Anzahl solcher Elektronen von dem entsprechenden Element abhängt ...**

(1.2) In a heat exchanger the gas mixture acquires the requisite temperature, the heat contained in the hot gas leaving the contact reactor (in which the above-mentioned reaction takes place in contact with the catalyst) being utilized to heat the incoming gas on its way to the reactor.
(HTW/II/TOWN-GAS DETOXICATION (CONVERSION OF CARBON MONOXIDE)/44)

(1.3) After etching, the remaining photoresist can be removed by a solvent, leaving a silicon substrate covered with $SiO_2$ only in the exposed areas.
(NSE/II/MICROSTRUCTURE FABRICATION (ELECTRONICS)/DESIGN/1851)

(1.4) The simplest kind of fuse is merely a length of thin wire which, in the event of a short circuit, is heated rapidly by ensuing high current and melts away, thus interrupting the circuit (Fig.1b). Fig.2 shows a more sophisticated fuse embodying this principle. The essential component is the fuse cartridge containing the fuse element (fusible wire or strip) embedded in sand. (HTW/I/SHORT-CIRCUIT (FUSE)/94)

(1.5) When a vibrating source of waves is approaching an observer, the frequency observed is higher than the frequency emitted by the source. When the source is receding, the observed frequency is lower than that emitted. (HTW/I/DOPPLER EFFECT/186)

**(2) The use of coordinate participles in a sentence**

(2.1) **Participles of the same type**

(2.1.1) Tabling. In this concentration process, a separation between two or more minerals is effected by flowing a pulp across a riffled plane surface **inclined** slightly from the horizontal, differentially **shaken** in the direction of the long axis, and **washed** with an even flow of water at right angles to the direction of motion.
(NSE/I/ CLASSIFYING (PROCESS)/647)

Notice that in **SE** a number of intransitive verbs, known as activo-passive verbs (cf. Gerbert 1970, 90), may be used transitively, in which case they have passive meanings. Mediopassive verbs - as they are also called -, such as **flow** in the sentence above, often correspond to '**lassen**' plus reflexive pronoun '**sich**' (or without the latter) in Ge.

Thus

"by <u>flowing</u> a pulp across a riffled plane surface"

should be interpreted as

"indem **man** eine Trübe über eine geriffelte ebene Oberfläche **fließen** läßt".

(2.1.2) The term "DATA" in the mathematical and technical sense denotes any facts or information, particularly as taken in, operated on, or put out by a computer or other machine for handling information. (HTW/I/DATA PROCESSING: PRINCIPLES/278)

(2.2) **Active and passive participles**

(2.2.1) A tuned amplifier, **employing** a transistor and **used** for the amplification of intermediate frequency signals, is shown in Fig.18.
(NSE/I/AMPLIFIER(TUNED AMPLIFIER)/143)

(2.2.2) A beam which is composed of two materials properly bonded together and having different moduli of elasticity is called a composite beam.
(NSE/I/BEAM(COMPOSITE)/335)

**(3) The repeated use of the same participial constructions in succession**

(3.1) The airspeed is generally measured by means of the airspeed indicator. It operates by utilising the pressure difference between static and dynamic air pressures, **the instrument usually being calibrated** to give readings in knots or in miles-per-hour. The dynamic pressure is produced in a so-called pitot tube (whose open end points in the direction of the flight), **the pressure difference being measured** by means of a diaphragm capsule. (HTW/I/AIR NAVIGATION/570)

(3.2) **When ignited,** hydrogen burns in air with a pale blue to colorless, nonluminous flame, yielding $H_20$. **When mixed with air**, the flammability limit is 4-74% hydrogen. **When mixed with oxygen**, the flammability limit is 4-94% hydrogen.
(NSE/I/HYDROGEN/1490)

### 2.3 Adjectival Constructions

Adjectives can sometimes be postpositive, i.e. they can immediately follow the noun or pronoun that they modify. In this case they can be regarded as **reduced relative clauses,** especially if they have postmodification or complementation themselves. The reduction can be considered to be the result of a two-step procedure: the relative pronoun and the respective form of '**be**' are replaced by the present participle **being**, which is deleted in the end, thus leaving only the adjective (with or without any complementation) in its postpositive place. Compare:

Negative valences **greater than four** do not occur.

This sentence can be reworded so as to make the underlying syntactic structure transparent:

Negative valences **being greater** than four ...

Negative valences **which are greater** than four...

In general En a few, partly semantic criteria must be taken account of for the adjective to be used in postposition. These are discussed in detail by Quirk et al. (1985, 418f) whose main points are summarized as follows:

(1) Postposition of the adjective is obligatory

(a) after compound indefinite pronouns and adverbs ending in **-body, -one, -thing, -where,** e.g.: "**Anyone** (who is) **intelligent** can do it";

(b) in several institutionalized expressions, mostly in official designations, such as **"the president elect"** (i.e. *'soon to take office'*).

(2) Adjectives ending in **-able** or **-ible** <u>can</u> have postposition

(a) when the preceding noun is modified by another adjective in the **superlative degree**, by **'only'**, or by the general ordinals **'last'**, **'next'**, etc., which implies the option of either attributive position or postposition, e.g.:

**"the best possible use"** vs **"the best use possible"**;

(b) when what they are denoting has only a *temporary* application, e.g.:

**"the visible stars"** vs **"the stars visible"** (i.e. *at a time specified or implied*).

(3) The four adjectives **absent, present, concerned** and **involved** are usually used postpositively when they designate *temporary* as opposed to *permanent* attributes, e.g.:
"The **men** (who were) **present** were his supporters".

In **SE** the use of postpositive adjectives undoubtedly goes beyond this set of rules, and adjectives with complementation in particular are far more common than in general En.

### 2.3.1 Postmodification of a Noun

A postpositive adjective that has no complementation allows of two options in Ge: It can either be shifted to **premodifying position** (a) or expressed as a **relative clause** (b). Compare:

(2.3.1.1) ... the reaction occurring within the detector will be limited only by the amount of **combustible gases or vapors present.** (NSE/I/GAS ANALYZERS/1291)
...die Reaktion, die in dem Analysegerät auftritt, wird nur durch die Menge
(a) **der vorhandenen brennbaren Gase oder Dämpfe** begrenzt.
(b) **der brennbaren Gase oder Dämpfe** begrenzt, **die vorhanden sind.**

(2.3.1.2) Of course the starting torque obtainable is inferior to that of a polyphase motor, but is sufficient to start a motor attached to a drive requiring low starting torque.
(NSE/II/SINGLE-PHASE MOTORS/1909)

(2.3.1.3) A beam which is continuous over several supports offers more difficulty in analysis than would a series of freely supported beams covering the same span. However, it can be analyzed readily by methods, classical or numerical, available for the analysis of statically indeterminate structures. (NSE/I/BEAM(STRUCTURAL)/336)

(2.3.1.4) In the high-temperature reactor the fuel elements are not clad in metal, the coolant is helium, and the power density attainable is as much as 10 MW/m.
(HTW/II/NUCLEAR REACTORS/32)

### 2.3.2 The Adjective as Relative Clause Equivalent

Adjectival constructions used in this function are frequently complemented by **(1) a prepositional phrase** or **(2) a to-infinitive clause**. As far as the former is concerned, the adjective occurs either with a preposition firmly attached to it, or with an optional one, depending on the context. Moreover, this type of adjectival constructions often shows the adjective in the **comparative degree (3).**

**(1) Complementation by a prepositional phrase**

(1.1) Alcohols with a large hydrocarbon group are found to have **physical properties similar to a hydrocarbon of the same structure.** (NSE/I/ALCOHOLS/79)
Man stellt fest, daß Alkohole mit einer großen Kohlenwasserstoffgruppe **physikalische Eigenschaften** haben, **die einem Kohlenwasserstoff mit gleicher Struktur ähnlich sind.** (or: ... **mit gleicher Struktur ähneln.**)

(1.2) To achieve a fuel management scheme with the lowest fuel cycle cost consistent with the current thermal and material performance limits, the following parameters are selected... (NSE/II/NUCLEAR POWER/FORT ST.VRAIN INSTALLATION/2008)

(1.3) Solid-state switches, capable of sampling signals at very high rates, normally are used in the analog multiplexer.
(NSE/I/HIGH-LEVEL ANALOG-INPUT SUBSYSTEMS/145)

(1.4) When the gain obtainable from a single amplifier is not sufficient for a given application, it is necessary to cascade two or more stages. (NSE/I/AMPLIFIER/139)

(1.5) The velocity attainable by the ions is governed by the difference in voltage along the path they have to traverse in the propulsion motor and by the charge and mass of the ions themselves. (HTW/II/ION-DRIVE ROCKET PROPULSION SYSTEMS/366)

(1.6) The highest frequencies attainable with a triode are in the region of about $10^4$ megahertz. (HTW/I/ULTRA-HIGH FREQUENCY VIBRATIONS/72)

Consider also:

blade elements close to the tip;
compressive stress parallel to the grain;
operating costs competitive with other traditional sources of energy;
steels comparable to those of heat-treated bars;
air pressure adjacent to the diaphragm;
specifying parameters applicable to incremental encoders;
the solvent preferential to the other components;
a data rate proportional to the total network data rate;
metallurgically bonded forms suitable for engineering applications;
superstructure only adequate for initial heat-up;

internal structures necessary for support of the core;
power available at the crankshaft;
stresses not exceeding those allowable at the temperatures;
packing densities now obtainable in microelectronic devices;
lands useful for production of foods;
the average percent defective for the process over the period;

control devices often automatic in operation;
the devices available for measuring radioactivity;
high temperature available from certain types of nuclear reactions;
large discharges possible in a high specific speed wheel.

**(2) Complementation by a to-infinitive clause**

(2.1) The work function can be considered to be **the total amount of work necessary to free an electron from a solid.** (NSE/I/ELECTRON TUBE/1046)
Die Austrittsarbeit kann als **der gesamte Arbeitsbetrag** betrachtet werden, **der notwendig ist, um ein Elektron aus einem Feststoff abzulösen.**

(2.2) Very large flares have been known to produce marked changes in the earth's geomagnetic field, which introduce electric currents in long-distance transmission lines strong enough to trip circuit breakers and to stop telegraph communication.
(NSE/II/SUN/FLARES/2729)

(2.3) Factor of safety has many different forms...It includes a combination of the allowances necessary to be made in the use of practical data, including an allowance for the lack of precision with which certain stress conditions can be ascertained.
(NSE/I/FACTOR OF SAFETY/1111)

**(3) The adjective in the comparative degree**

(3.1) A number of basic discoveries were made. For example, finding that the property of superconductivity could be destroyed by the application of **a magnetic field equal to or greater than a critical field $H_c$.**
(NSE/II/SUPERCONDUCTIVITY RESEARCH/2734)
Es wurde eine Anzahl grundlegender Entdeckungen gemacht. Zum Beispiel die Feststellung, daß die Eigenschaft der Supraleitfähigkeit durch die Anwendung **eines magnetischen Feldes, das gleich oder größer als ein kritisches Feld $H_c$** ist, zerstört werden könnte.

(3.2) The system is designed for an outside temperature somewhat higher than that of the coldest day of the year, assuming the need for boosting from other sources for a few days each year. (NSE/I/GEOTHERMAL ENERGY IN ICELAND/1320)

(3.3) The instrument sometimes is proportioned so that the numbering begins with unity at the top, being applicable only to liquids heavier than water.
(NSE/II/SPECIFIC GRAVITY/HAND HYDROMETER/2651)

(3.4) When the saturated solution of a substance in water has a water vapor pressure greater than that of the surrounding atmosphere, evaporation of the water from solution takes place. (NSE/I/EFFLORESCENCE/993)

### 2.3.3 The Adjective as Adverbial Clause Equivalent

In section 2.2.2.6 mention has already been made that in **SE** verbless clauses are particularly indicative of reduced adjective clauses, which, indeed, have much in common with reduced participial constructions in that they can be used as

(1) **related** adjective clauses, in which the implied subject is identical with that of the main clause, as well as

(2) **absolute** adjective clauses, in which the covert participle has its own overt subject.

Related adjective clauses are primarily used in initial and medial positions, whereas absolute adjective clauses are employed in final position.

**(1) The related adjective clause**

Few examples can be given showing this adjectival construction without the use of a subordinating conjunction (1.1), while the majority of the ascertained sample sentences show the related adjective clause with a conjunction preceding it (1.2), which suggests the necessity of avoiding misunderstanding.

**(1.1) The related adjective clause used without a conjunction**

(1.1.1) **Indicative of a genetic deficiency** or mutation of some kind, **albino redwoods** are uncommon, but not rare.
(NSE/II/REDWOOD (COAST)/GENETIC RESEARCH/2415)

The two-step procedure for the identification of reduced relative clauses, described at the beginning of section 2.3, can also be applied in order to make the nature of the reduced adverbial clause transparent, although, admittedly, there may be more scope for the interpretation of the semantic relationship conveyed.

Compare:

**Although being indicative of a genetic deficiency ..., albino redwoods** are uncommon ...

**Although they are indicative of a genetic deficiency ..., albino redwoods** are uncommon ...

(1.1.2) Typical of the elliptical galaxy, this object shows no evidence of recent star formation and little or no gas between the stars. (NSE/I/ELLIPTICAL GALAXIES/1275)

(1.1.3) Difficult to comprehend for all but the older readers, the early days of flying were indeed thrilling times... (NSE/I/HISTORICAL AIRCRAFT/EARLY HISTORY/73)

**(1.2) The related adjective clause preceded by a conjunction**

(1.2.1) Concentration cells, **although interesting theoretically**, are not important commercially. (NSE/I/GALVANIC CELL/1283)
Konzentrationszellen sind technisch nicht wichtig, **obwohl sie theoretisch interessant sind.**

(1.2.2) The fast breeder, even though costly to build, does offer several temptations. (NSE/II/FAST BREEDER REACTORS IN PERSPECTIVE/2017)

(1.2.3) If this normal stress is tensile, it is often called a diagonal tension stress; if compressive it is known as a diagonal compression stress.
(NSE/II/STRESS (STRUCTURAL)/2790)

(1.2.4) When pure, the metal is soft and malleable, but must be worked and fabricated under inert gas atmosphere. (NSE/II/SAMARIUM/2497)

(1.2.5) Although more costly to operate, the electric-furnace process produces phosphoric acid of high purity. (NSE/II/PHOSPHORIC ACID/2189)

**(2) The absolute adjective clause**

(2.1) This type of verbless clause, although not uncommon, seems to be extremely rare in **SE**. Compare:

(2.1.1) It is now in order to state the nature of elementary streamline patterns and explain how a complex pattern may be considered the result of the addition of two potential forces, **each capable of producing a different character of streamline** in the same region. (NSE/I/AERODYNAMICS AND AEROSTATICS/STREAMLINE PATTERNS/45)
Es ist jetzt an der Zeit, die Beschaffenheit elementarer Stromlinienmuster zu besprechen und zu erkären, wie ein komplexes Muster als Ergebnis der Addition von zwei potentiellen Kräften betrachtet werden kann, **wobei jede in der Lage ist, eine unterschiedliche Stromlinienart** in dem gleichen Bereich **zu erzeugen**.

(2.1.2) The core auxiliary cooling system consisted of two redundant cooling loops, each capable of removing 100% of the afterheat, for the 2000 MWt plant and three redundant cooling loops, each capable of removing 50% of the decay heat, for the 3000 MWt plant. (NSE/II/NUCLEAR POWER/LARGE COMMERCIAL HTGRs/2010)

(2.2) **'with' + object + adjective**

Remember what has been stated with regard to this special variant of absolute constructions in sections 2.2.2.6/(2) and 2.2.4.6/(2.2).

(2.2.1) The drag is also increased, giving a steeper gliding angle with flap down than without the use of the flap. Apart from any disadvantage, this factor may actually be beneficial since **with flap position variable** and under control of the pilot, the angle of normal gliding is alterable. (NSE/I/HIGH-LIFT-DEVICES/47)

## 2.4 Infinitival Constructions

### 2.4.1 Postmodification of a Noun

Like the participles and the adjective, the infinitive can be used as a postmodifier so that it can be regarded as being equivalent to a relative clause, and, like the former, may be used with or without any complementation. In **SE** the dominant construction is the passive infinitive clause (1) while the active counterpart (2) is less common.

**(1) The passive infinitive as relative clause substitute**

This construction results from omitting the **relative pronoun** and the respective form of **'be'.** It usually has a *modal* sense. *Modality* as well as *tense* and *mood* have to be inferred from the infinitive clause. The variety of implicit *tense*, *modality*, and *mood* is illustrated by Quirk et al. (1985, 1267f) as follows:

| | |
|---|---|
| The case **to be investigated** tomorrow... | ('that **will**, or **is to, be investigated'**) |
| The animals **to be found** in Kenya... | ('that **can be**, or **are found'**) |
| The procedure **to be followed...** | ('that **must**, or **should,** or **will, be followed'**) |

Compare:

(1.1) **The metal objects to be enamelled** are heated thoroughly, pickled in acid, neutralised in alkaline bath, and rinsed.(HTW/I/ENAMEL/350)

Notice that the implied *modality* can be made explicit in Ge:

> **Die Gegenstände** aus metallischem Werkstoff, **die emailliert werden sollen,** werden sorgfältig erwärmt, in Säure gebeizt, in einem Alkalibad neutralisiert und dann abgespühlt.

Or alternatively a mixed structure consisting of present participle and infinitive can be chosen:

> Die **zu emaillierenden** Gegenstände aus metallischem Werkstoff...

(1.2) Screw threads can be produced ... by mechanical methods which comprise turning (on a lathe), milling, rolling, pressing or casting. Which of these methods is most suitable in any particular case will depend on the number of screw-threaded components to be produced, the desired precision of the thread, and the quality of surface finish to be obtained. (HTW/II/SCREW CUTTING/158)

(1.3) Cylindrical-coordinate robots are often well suited where tasks to be performed or machines to be serviced are located radially from the robot and where no obstructions are present. (NSE/II/CLASSIFICATION OF ROBOTS/AXES OF MOTION/2453)

(1.4) Essentially, the device is a mosaic-image sensor, or a mosaic of photocells onto which each character to be read by the system is focused.
(NSE/II/OPTICAL CHARACTER RECOGNITION(OCR)/2080)

(1.5) Chlorine is combined with zinc to a salt at an activating electrode on discharge and formed as a gas to be transported to and stored in another location as a solid hydrate, on charge. (NSE/I/BATTERY/GAS ELECTRODES/332)

**(2) The active infinitive as relative clause substitute**

In this construction, in which the antecedent corresponds to the subject of the infinitive, the interpretation may be *nonmodal*, especially if the antecedent is used with general ordinals, such as **last, only,** and **first** (cf. sentence (2.2) below). Apart from that, the implied sense may also be that of *purpose*, which can be made explicit in Ge. Compare:

(2.1) **The gas to drive the turbine** may be produced in a gas generator by the decomposition of hydrogen peroxide by means of a catalyst.
(HTW/II/LIQUID-PROPELLANT ROCKET SYSTEMS/362)
**Das Gas, das die Turbine antreibt,** kann in einem Gasgenerator durch die Zersetzung des Wasserstoffperoxids mit Hilfe eines Katalysators erzeugt werden.
**Das Gas für den Antrieb der Turbine** ...

(2.2) In 1935, Domagk, a German researcher, was **the first to observe the clinical value of prontosil,** a red compound derived from azo dyes. Paraaminobenzenesulfonamide was shown to be the effective portion of the prontosil molecule. This substance was given the name, sulfanilamide. This was **the first of a group of related drugs to receive wide clinical trial**. (NSE/II/SULFONAMIDE DRUGS/2718)

(2.3) A sufficiently powerful airflow to carry along dust and grit particles must be set up.
(HTW/I/VACUUM CLEANER/258)

(2.4) A clarifying agent to assist in this operation must possess certain properties for acting on the suspended particles - chemical precipitation, attractive via ionic forces, absorption qualities (large surface areas plus weak forces).
(NSE/I/CLARIFYING AGENTS/646)

### 2.4.2 Object Complementation by an Infinitive Clause

The infinitive clause in this construction has no subject itself, but its implied subject is the **preceding noun phrase**, which is object of the superordinate clause, or, put in another way, the noun phrase functions syntactically as object of the superordinate clause and has semantically the role of subject of the infinitive clause. This may be illustrated as follows:

| | The difference in pressure | causes | the airplane | to roll. |
|---|---|---|---|---|
| **Syntactically** | S | P | 0 | C(inf) |
| **Semantically:** | S | P | S | (P) |

This sentence can be put down to two independent clauses, the latter giving evidence of the close *syntactic-semantic link* between "the airplane" and "to roll":

The difference in pressure causes trouble. The airplane is rolling.

The complement of the object may be either a to-infinitive or a bare infinitive, depending on the semantic nature of the verb functioning as predicate. The verbs allowing the object plus to-infinitive complementation may be semantically subdivided into the following groups:

(a) ***Factual*** verbs, i.e. verbs that denote activities such as *thinking, saying, reporting* and *planning*, e.g.

**assume, believe, claim, consider, design, estimate, expect, feel** (in Ge = verstehen), **find, imagine, know, report, show, take,** etc. Note that **say** cannot take object plus infinitive complementation.

The nonfinite construction following these verbs can often be replaced by an object clause, introduced by the conjunction **'that'** = Ge **'daß'**. Compare:

The engineer **reported the building site (to be) in a good position.**

The engineer reported **that the building site was in a good position.**

Some scientists **believe the irrigation project (to be) incomplete.**

Some scientists believe **that the irrigation project is incomplete.**

With *factual* verbs like these, the nonfinite clause normally contains a verb of *stative* meaning, such as '**be**'. Notice, however, that quite a few *factual* verbs may be used without '**be**', e.g. **believe, consider, prove, report, suppose,** and **think.**

(b) *Causative* verbs, i.e. verbs that show that something brings about or causes an *action* or a *resultant state.* In **SE** this group of verbs includes also verbs which normally express concepts such as *enablement, permission and compulsion,* e.g.

**allow, cause, command, compel, force, enable, lead, permit,** etc.

The verbs allowing the object plus bare infinitive complementation include a relative small number of *causative* verbs, namely **let, make** (= Ge 'veranlassen') and **have** ( = Ge 'veranlassen').

(c) Other semantic groups of verbs, such as *volitional* verbs like **wish** and **want**, taking the to-infinitive, and *perceptual* verbs like **hear** and **watch,** taking the bare infinitive, are negligible in **SE**, except the *volitional* verb **require** and the *perceptual* verb **see**.

The object plus infinitive complementation may be identical with the Ge structure, especially if it occurs after *causative* verbs. Compare:

The car mechanic **made the engine run** to find the cause of erratic running.
Der Autoschlosser **ließ den Motor laufen**, um die Ursache für den unruhigen Lauf des Motors zu finden.

The other Ge alternative is usually an object clause, introduced almost always by **'daß'**. Compare:

| These factors | cause | the condensation | to take one form or another. |
|---|---|---|---|
| S | P | O | C(inf) **with/without 'to'** |
| Diese Faktoren | **verursachen,** | **daß die Kondensation** die eine oder andere Form **aufweist**. | |

This version reflects the semantic function of the object, illustrated at the beginning of this section.

Notice that some *causative* verbs, e.g. **have, make** (=Ge **'veranlassen'**), and **allow** (= Ge '**(zu)lassen**'), may take object plus participle complementation.

Compare: It is necessary **to have the cages rotating**.

Es ist notwendig, **die Käfige rotieren zu lassen.**

A brittle material **may have its useful life terminated** by a sudden blow.

**Die Lebensdauer** eines spröden Werkstoffes **kann** durch einen plötzlichen Schlag **beendet werden**.

For the uses of this construction see the examples in sections 2.2.2.4/(2.2) and 2.2.4.4/(2).

In **SE** object complementation by an infinitive clause is relatively frequent after *causative* verbs. This fact will be taken account of in the choice of examples. Note, too, that the infinitive may occur both in the active and passive form. Compare:

(2.4.2.1) In the absence of discontinuities, for instance in vacuum, **one expects these values to differ** by infinitesimal amounts if the corresponding points are infinitesimally close, in some way which is typical of the field considered; ... (NSE/I/FIELD THEORY/1141)
Bei nicht vorhandenen Diskontinuitäten, zum Beispiel im Vakuum, **erwartet man, daß sich diese Werte** durch infinitesimale Beträge **unterscheiden**, wenn die entsprechenden Punkte infinitesimal dicht aneinanderliegen, und zwar in einer Weise, die typisch für das betrachtete Feld ist; ...

(2.4.2.2) The piperidyl benzilate esters and phenylcyclohexyl piperidines are synthetic compounds, and have not been shown to occur naturally. Some authorities do not consider them to be hallucinogens, but active researchers in the field include them among the most active psychotomimetics (NSE/I/HALLUCINOGENS/1401)

(2.4.2.3) Localized buckling of the web must be resisted in order to permit the web to develop its full strength. (NSE/I/GIRDER/1337)

(2.4.2.4) At the best speed the final velocity will be just sufficient to enable the water to clear the runner. (NSE/I/HYDRAULIC TURBINES/1465)

(2.4.2.5) The target is to have the material arrive at the blast furnace, after prior handling, with about 85-90% of the material over 1/4 inch.
(NSE/I/IRON ORE PROCESSING/BENEFICIATION/1601)

(2.4.2.6) A rotating impeller mounted in a casing and revolved at high speed will cause a fluid which is continuously admitted near the center of rotation to experience an outward flow and a pressure rise due to centrifugal action.
(NSE/I/AIR COMPRESSION/CENTRIFUGAL COMPRESSORS/60)

(2.4.2.7) The objective of automation is to cause the work system to be as automatic, i.e., self-acting, self-regulating, and self-reliant, as may be possible - but against the real and practical backdrop of various economic, environmental, social, and other reasons.
(NSE/I/AUTOMATION/288)

(2.4.2.8) The volume that is displaced by these two piston movements is, however, the same in both cylinders, i.e., the small piston has to travel a great distance to make the large piston move only a short distance. (HTW/I/PRESSES/18)

(2.4.2.9) This preheating of the gas and air enables the combustion temperature of the flame to be considerably raised. (HTW/I/STEEL/334)

(2.4.2.10) In other words, a suction is developed there, which causes the petrol to be sucked out of the choke tube and be atomised.(HTW/I/CARBURETTOR/478)

(2.4.2.11) To enable the sulphides to be reduced with carbon or dissolved with dilute acid, total or partial removal of the sulphur is necessary.
(HTW/II/ROASTING OF ORES AND CONCENTRATES/94)

(2.4.2.12) It is the commutator that requires the rotor to be the armature so that coils and their switching arrangement always move exactly together.
(NSE/I/DIRECT-CURRENT CIRCUITS/918)

### 2.4.3 "for" plus Object Complementation by an Infinitive Clause

The object, complemented by an infinitive clause, may be introduced by the preposition **for**, which usually occurs with adjectives (e.g. **necessary for**), adverbs (e.g. the engine is running too **fast for**), verbs (e.g. **provide for**) and nouns (e.g. **time for**). The preposition **for**, however, is not seen to be dependent on any of these word classes, as is evident by the initial position of the '**for-construction**' in sentences such as

**For man to survive** in space...

What matters is that the preposition **for** makes with the following object and infinitive clause a particularly close syntactic-semantic group by introducing the logical subject of the action denoted by the infinitive. "After **for** the infinitive has the advantage of avoiding tenses while being clear and precise at the same time" (Sager/Dungworth 1980, 1085). In **SE** this construction is preferably used as an economic tool for reducing finite clauses of *purpose,* introduced, for instance, by **in order that** (Ge **damit**) or **so that** (Ge **so daß).** The '**for-construction**' may also correspond to an *object* clause or, in particular, if it is used in initial position (cf. Gerbert 1970, 65f), a *conditional* or *infinitive* clause in Ge. Compare:

(2.4.3.1) In adaptive control, **a method must be provided for the system to change parameters** automatically within the closed loop. (NSE/I/ADAPTIVE CONTROL/32)
Bei der Adaptivregelung **muß eine Methode sicherstellen, daß das System die Parameter** in dem Kreis mit Rückführung automatisch **ändert.**

(2.4.3.2) **Correct processing involves heating the plastic sufficiently for it to flow freely** (not forcing half-melted plastic through a die or into a mold) and cooling it slowly. (NSE/I/CELLULOSE/PROCESSING/521)

**Richtige Verarbeitung beinhaltet ausreichende Erwärmung des Kunststoffes, damit er frei fließen kann,** (und nicht das Drücken von halb geschmolzenem Kunststoff durch eine Düse oder in eine Preßform) und seine langsame Abkühlung.

(2.4.3.3) ... the galaxy as it is currently observed is at a point in its developmental history such that there has not been sufficient time for the gas to dissipate; (NSE/I/ELLIPTICAL GALAXIES/1276)

(2.4.3.4) It is generally understood that for a laser to serve as a weapon it must have appropriate wavelength and brightness characteristics (NSE/II/X-RAY AND OTHER VERY HIGH-POWER LASERS/1676)

(2.4.3.5) For an amplifier to be classed as stable, on the other hand, the initial transients must decay with time. (NSE/I/FEEDBACK/1115)

(2.4.3.6) For the engine to operate properly, it is necessary that the vibratory resonance of the air inlet valves be "tuned" with the impulses of the gases and sound waves escaping from the nozzle. (NSE/I/PULSEJET ENGINE/66)

Notice that **'in order for'** may occcasionally be found to substitute **'for'**, as shown in the following two examples. Compare:

(2.4.3.7) The fuel must be heated to a temperature of $10^8$ Celsius degrees in order for the nuclei to overcome strong electrostatic repulsion and get close enough to fuse. (NSE/I/FUSION POWER/ TEMPERATURE AND CONFINEMENT/1263)

(2.4.3.8) In order for a transformer to deliver secondary emf, the primary emf must vary with respect to time. (NSE/II/FUNDAMENTALS OF TRANSFORMER/2852)

#### 2.4.4 Subject Complementation by an Infinitive Clause

This construction is the result of the passivization of the object plus infinitive complementation, discussed in section 2.4.2. Passivization, which shifts the object into subject position, entails the use of the to-infinitive.

The subject plus infinitive complementation can be used with all the semantic groups of verbs taking the object plus infinitive complementation, including **say, see** and the verb of *intention*, **mean.** In **SE** it is very common because it is stylistically neutral and enables the writer or speaker "to report new developments in research and industry without expressing his own opinion about the validity of claims made by manufacturers or other interested parties" (Sager et al. 1980, 213). That explains the large variety of *factual* verbs, used in this construction, although *causative* verbs, for instance, are by no means infrequent.

Ge equivalent constructions include impersonal expressions of the type "**Es heißt, daß**...", the impersonal pronoun "**man**", e.g. "**Man erwartet, daß**...", or **passive** structures, e.g. "**Es wird vermutet, daß...**".

Compare:

(2.4.4.1) **Positive electrons, or positrons are** now **known (1) to occur** as decay products from certain radioactive isotopes, (2) **to be produced** (paired with a negative electron) in certain interactions of high-energy gamma rays with intense electric fields near nuclei, and (3) **to be the product** of certain decays of certain mesons.
(NSE/I/POSITIVE ELECTRONS/1045)
**Es ist jetzt bekannt, daß positive Elektronen oder Positronen** (1) als Zerfallsprodukte aus bestimmten radioaktiven Isotopen **vorkommen,** (2) paarweise mit einem negativen Elektron in bestimmten Wechselwirkungen energiereicher Gammastrahlung mit starken elektrischen Feldern in der Nähe der Kerne **erzeugt werden** und (3) **das Produkt** eines gewissen Zerfalls bestimmter Mesonen **sind**.

(2.4.4.2) The system is now said to be in a state of resonance.
(HTW/II/RESONANCE AND ENGINE EFFICIENCY/274)

(2.4.4.3) The fourth power of the receiving surface temperature is thus seen to be small compared to the fourth power of the transmitting surface temperature.
(NSE/I/HEAT TRANSFER/1427)

(2.4.4.4) Alcohols with a large hydrocarbon group are found to have physical properties similar to a hydrocarbon of the same nature. (NSE/II/ALCOHOLS/79)

(2.4.4.5) Primary cells are meant to be discharged to exhaustion only once and then discarded.
(NSE/I/BATTERY/328)

(2.4.4.6) The counter counts down to "zero" and, at a determined position, the motor is commanded to slow down. (NSE/I/INCREMENTAL ENCODER/1063)

(2.4.4.7) If the center of pressure were permitted to travel during angle of attack variations, pitching moments would be introduced into the rotor system; this condition would set up violent vibrations. (NSE/I/AIRFOIL SECTION/1430)

(2.4.4.8) Conversion of an existing natural gas line to hydrogen service is estimated to require a rise of compressor capacity by a factor of 3.8 and compressor horsepower by 5.5.
(NSE/I/HYDROGEN AS AN ENERGY TRANSPORTER/1496)

(2.4.4.9) Several essential amino acids have been shown to be the limiting factor of nutrition in plant proteins. (NSE/I/AMINO ACIDS/124)

(2.4.4.10) ... brittle fractures have been known to travel as far as half a mile in welded gas pipelines, often with extremely high velocities. (NSE/I/BRITTLE FRACTURE/443)

(2.4.4.11) Laser-induced processes are expected to increase in number and expand in application, but the principal obstacle to large-scale introduction of the laser into the chemical industry is an economic one. (NSE/II/LASER CHEMISTRY/2198)

(24.4.12) Although a streamtube is ordinarily imagined to have a circular cross section, it will be convenient here to think of a streamtube having a rectangular cross section. (NSE/I/AERODYNAMICS AND AEROSTATICS/STREAMTUBE/45)

(2.4.4.13) The energy that is released when steam expands is made to produce rotary motion which can be used for the driving of machinery. (HTW/I/STEAM ENGINE/28)

(2.4.4.14) The camera operator was required only to focus and press the shutter release after programing the film speed into the camera. (NSE/II/ PHOTOGRAPHY AND IMAGERY/EXPOSURE METERING SYSTEMS /2207)

(2.4.4.15) Moreover, by controlling the architecture of the LB film, the interactions can be designed to be of a lock-key type, thus enhancing the selectivity of the device. (NSE/II/MOLECULAR AND SUPERMOLECULAR ELECTRONICS/PROMISING APPLIED RESEARCH AREAS/(C)SENSORS/1879)

(2.4.4.16) ...some additives in the past have been found to be damaging to health. (NSE/I/ADDITIVES(FOOD)/37)

Notice that in this type of complementation **find** can be used without **'be'** if the following word is an **adjective**. Compare:

(2.4.4.17) Irregularity of the plate, poor surface graining, "trees", insufficient bond, and other trouble develop. The overcoming of these requires the use of various expedients, such as careful control of temperature, or the addition of certain colloids and other compounds which have been found effective in preventing formation of defects on the plated article. (NSE/I/ELECTROPLATING/1048)

The multiple use of infinitival constructions is illustrated in the following example, which shows a short text consisting of two sentences. As to the interpretation of the second sentence, remember also what has been stated in section 2.4.2.

(2.4.4.18) This emission of electrons from an incandescent metal (usually an electrically heated filament) can most suitably be made to take place in a vacuum. This prevents oxidation of the very hot surface of the metal and allows the electrons to emerge unobstructed, i,e., without colliding with, or being neutralised by, gas molecules and ions of the air. (HTW/I/THERMIONIC(VACUUM)TUBE/70)

## 3. THE PHENOMENON OF SYNTACTIC CLUSTERS

In the preceding paragraphs the focus has been on various devices of clause reduction, which are considered to be characteristic of scientific and technical communication. Each of them has been described and interpreted at various levels, in syntactic, lexicogrammatical and semantic terms, by drawing upon authentic sentences or even short extracts or sample texts, if the sentential context did not provide the clues necessary for the comprehension and/or interpretation of the constructions concerned. These devices, however, do not only occur as separate units in a sentence, but often closely co-occur, so that the resulting text configurations may become rather complex, together with the relatively high lexical density, i.e. the number of lexical items per clause, as will be discussed and illustrated below.

What Halliday (1988, 163) describes as "the prototypical syndrome of features that characterizes scientific English" should be interpreted so as to imply also those syntactic features that are due to the large number of clause-reducing devices, which, like any other items of text production in **SE**, can be shown to have clusters of related features. It is on this condition that Halliday's conclusion after a thorough text analysis of two sentences can be agreed to: "...it is the combined effect of a number of such related features and the relations they contract throughout the text as a whole, rather than the obligatory presence of any particular ones, that tells us that what is being constructed is the discourse of science" (ibidem, 164).

The tendency to prefer clause-reducing devices in **SE** may not only bring about some difficulty in inferring the semantic relationship of, say, the related participle clause (cf. section 2.2.2.6), for instance, but may also result in an extremly high intricacy of sentence structure, depending on the number and nature of nonfinite clause structures and their interdependencies in the sentence. This may lead to what can be called **syntactic clusters** (=Ge **syntaktische Kombinationen**) by which I mean '**clause-reducing devices which are deliberately grouped together or occur close together so that they become interlinked**' (cf. Baakes 1967, 20). It goes without saying that difficulties of interpretation are bound to arise, unless the constructions involved are well known and experience in sentence analysis permits the correct identification of the kind of relationship existing between them.

Compare:

> In its original and strict sense the term "annealing" describes **the process of heating an alloy and allowing it to cool in the furnace.**
> In seinem ursprünglichen und genauen Sinn beschreibt der Terminus "Glühen" **den Vorgang des Erwärmens einer Legierung und ihrer Abkühlung** (*des Abkühlenlassens) im Ofen.

In the course of translating this sentence irritation may be felt as soon as **allowing** comes into focus. From what has been said about the use of the gerund in section 2.1.3/(2) it follows that **allowing** is a gerund depending on the preposition **of** in the NP "**...the process of...**", in the same way as **heating** is dependent on it. The ability to realize this kind of syntactic relationship is prerequisite to understanding the conveyed message and its wording in Ge. This is what I wrote by way of explanation (ibid. 1967):

"Dieses Beispiel läßt sich nicht mit den erwähnten Übersetzungsmöglichkeiten übertragen, da die Form '**allowing**' hier nicht, wie gewöhnlich, Prädikat ist (refer back to section 2.4.2), sondern ein Gerundium, das wie '**heating**' als Attribut zu '**process**' steht. Daher kann der folgende 0.m.I. (= En object complementation by an infinitive clause) wie '**an alloy**' nur substantivisch übersetzt werden."

The following example shows that the verb taking the object plus infinitive complementation is a present participle, used to reduce a sentential relative clause (cf. section 2.2.2.5/pp 63-64).

> The tubes are so connected that the water or internal fluid makes several passes up and down the exchanger, **thus enabling a high velocity to be obtained** for a given heat-transfer area and given throughput of liquid.
> Die Rohre sind so verbunden, daß das Wasser oder die innere Flüssigkeit im Austauscher mehrere Durchgänge auf und nieder macht, **was auf diese Weise ermöglicht, daß eine hohe Fließgeschwindigkeit** für ein gegebenes Wärmeübertragungsgebiet und einen gegebenen Durchsatz der Flüssigkeit **erzielt werden kann.**

The result of the analysis of these two sentences gives rise to the assumption that infinitival constructions are frequently involved in **syntactic clusters.** This assumption is indeed well-founded, as will become evident when making an in-depth study of the following examples.

Compare:

(3.1) In addition, making fusion work is so difficult that, if anything goes wrong with the reaction, the process simply stops. (NSE/I/FUSION POWER/1263)

(3.2) In most systems, all load and unload as well as refixturing operations must be done at special stations and not on the machine tools themselves. Thus, each refixturing requires the part leaving a machine, traveling to a special station, and then traveling back again to continue being machined.
(NSE/II/DESIGNING FOR NC PRODUCTION/2037)

(3.3) The squirrel-cage motor is a particular type of induction motor. Such motors are in general characterized by having only the stator connected to the external circuit.
(HTW/II/ALTERNATING-CURRENT MACHINES/512)

(3.4) Because of the elliptical shape of the earth's orbit, the sun as seen by a geocentric observer moves with varying angular velocity in the course of a year. Since the eccentricity of the orbit is only slight, this variation can adequately be simulated by causing the earth, represented by a pin, to rotate with constant angular velocity on a disc whose axis of rotation corresponds to the E-axis, while the sun is given a fixed amount of eccentricity. (HTW/II/PLANETARIUM/396)

(3.5) A number of oxides of lead are known, but not all are daltonide compounds. Thus, lead(I) oxide, $Pb_20$, made by heating lead(II) oxalate, has been shown by x-ray analysis to be a mixture of the metal and lead(II) oxide, Pb0. The latter is obtained by heating lead in air, which yields a yellow, rhombic material, which has a peculiar layer structure having each lead atom attached to four oxygen atoms all lying on the same side of it, forming a square pyramid with the lead at the apex.
(NSE/II/LEAD/CHEMISTRY OF LEAD/1687)

(3.6) The Luft detector operates similarly, but the detector has two chambers separated by a diaphragm. ... Having separate chambers does, however, allow for the possibility of a change occurring in one-half of the detector and not the other and thus resulting in zero drift. (NSE/I/MICROPHONE DETECTORS/1552)

(3.7) To reduce the number of cables required, digital loop carrier systems use digital multiplexing and transmission techniques, thereby enabling a number of customer loops to share a smaller number of wire pairs and electronics.
(NSE/II/LOCAL TELEPHONE LOOP/2778)

(3.8) This valve closes the pipe leading from the main air reservoir to the main brake pipe. At the same time another valve is opened whereby the pressure is released from the main brake pipe, thus causing the brakes to be applied, the effect being the same as if the brake valve had been actuated. (HTW/I/RAILWAY SAFETY DEVICES/532)

(3.9) When one flap is opened, the ridge on its cam slides under a projection on the push-rod under it, thus locking the push-rod and preventing the other flaps from being opened. (HTW/I/AUTOMATIC VENDING MACHINES/326)

(3.10) In the locked position (Fig 1) a number of pin tumblers of different lengths and comprising an upper and lower segment are pressed down by springs to engage with holes in the cylinder, thereby preventing the latter from rotating. (HTW/I/CYLINDER LOCK/234)

(3.11) Instead, it is necessary to have a wound rotor, i.e., a rotor provided with a winding connected to slip rings, enabling variable resistors (rheostats) to be connected in series. (HTW/II/ALTERNATING-CURRENT MACHINES/514)

(3.12) The combustion of fuel in an internal combustion engine is not a continuous affair, but a series of individual explosions, each one requiring a metered amount of fuel to be individually ignited. (NSE/I/INTERNAL COMBUSTION ENGINE/1581)

(3.13) In other processes for welded tube manufacture the skelp is shaped in the cold condition, only the edges of the slot being heated to enable the weld to be formed. (HTW/I/ROLLING MILL MANUFACTURE OF TUBULAR PRODUCTS/340)

(3.14) Whereas chemical-propellant rockets are characterised by high thrust for short durations and are therefore more particularly suitable for getting large payloads launched from the ground, electrical propulsion systems have been proposed which would yield a relatively low thrust over a long period of time. (HTW/I/ROCKETS/580)

(3.15) This distribution of cosmic rays correlates well with the region of highest concentration of supernova remnants and pulsars - the latter believed also to have resulted from supernovae. (NSE/I/GAMMA-RAY ASTRONOMY/1286)

(3.16) Consider the familiar electrodynamic transducer. A periodic electric current passing through a coil interacts with a steady magnet flux causing the coil to vibrate. The coil in turn drives a diaphragm which radiates sound waves from one side. ... The entire process is reversible since sound waves striking the diaphragm set up a periodic variation in air pressure adjacent to the diaphragm causing it to vibrate. (NSE/I/ELECTROACOUSTICS/23)

(3.17) ION IMPLANTATION. A process for introducing alloying elements into a host material by accelerating the ions to a high energy (at least tens of kilovolts) and allowing them to strike the surface of the host. (NSE/I/ION IMPLANTATION/1595)

(3.18) These agents operate in connection with mechanical equipment to bring about the removal of suspended particles that represent product impurities. Allowing such particles to settle by gravity alone would require very long periods. (NSE/I/CLARIFYING AGENTS/646)

(3.19) Strain gauges can be used for a variety of technical and scientific purposes involving the measurement of small amounts of deformation or displacement. Thus, a specially shaped strain gauge affixed to a diaphragm enables the deformations of the diaphragm, and therefore of the magnitude of the pressure acting on it, to be measured. (HTW/II/ELECTRIC-RESISTANCE STRAIN GAUGE/480)

(3.20) Intensification of the frictional effect in conjunction with an increase in power input causes the actual mixing effect to diminish in importance as compared with the comminuting (or disintegrating) effect associated with friction. (HTW/II/MIXING OF MATERIALS/498)

(3.21) Astronomical aircraft navigation is done with the aid of the astro-compass, which is a non-magnetic instrument which enables the true heading of an aircraft to be found by sighting upon a celestial body. (HTW/I/AIR NAVIGATION/570)

(3.22) At first believed to be caused by moonlets, the final conclusion drawn was that the fluctuations were caused by the presence of rings. (NSE/II/URANUS IN PERSPECTIVE/2901)

(3.23) Next, the refrigerant is condensed, giving off heat in the process, and then made to evaporate again. (HTW/I/REFRIGERATORS/256)

(3.24) The projector is a "universal instrument" in the sense that it can be made to show the night sky as seen from any place on the earth's surface, and not only as it appears at the present time, but also at any time in the distant past or the distant future. (HTW/II/PLANETARIUM/392)

(3.25) The resonance frequency depends upon the strength of the transverse field. Thus, a thin film of a ferromagnetic substance placed in a static magnetic field **H** is found to be capable of absorbing from an oscillating field whose magnetic vector is perpendicular to **H** at a frequency given by $w = \left(\frac{ge}{2mc}\right)\sqrt{BH}$ where **B** is the magnetic induction associated with **H**, **e** and **m** are the charge and the mass of the electron, **c** is the velocity of light, and **g** is very near to 2, the Landé factor for free electrons. (NSE/I/FERROMAGNETISM/1127)

The phenomenon of **syntactic clusters** has been explained as being the result of an extremely high density of interrelated nonfinite clause structures. It can therefore be regarded as an outstanding characteristic among the distinguishing features of **ESL** (cf. section 1.2), which, together with the terminologies of the special subject fields of Science and Technology, largely make up the difference between **SE** and general English.

## BIBLIOGRAPHY


Allen, J. P. Widdowson, H. G. (1 974). English in Physical Science. Oxford: OUP.

Baakes, K. (1967). Wichtige syntaktische Erscheinungen im technischen Englisch. Magdeburg: TH-Druck.

Baakes, K. (1984). Theorie und Praxis der Terminologieforschung. Deutsch - Englisch. Am Beispiel der Umformtechnik in der Metallbearbeitung. Heidelberg: Julius Groos Verlag.

Baakes, K. (1992). A Communicative Approach to Teaching Terminology in ESP. In: Special Language/Fachsprache 1-2, pp 23-41.

Bald, W.-D. (1988). Kernprobleme der englischen Grammatik. Berling-Schöneberg: Langenscheidt-Longman.

Beier, R. (1980). Englische Fachsprache. Stuttgart: VerlagW. Kohlhammer.

Benson, M./Benson, E./Ilson, R. (1986). The BBI Combinatory Dictionary of English. A Guide to Word Combinations. Amsterdam/Philadelphia: John Benjamins Publishing Company.

Black, B.J. (1981). Manufacturing technology for level-3 technicians. Colchester and London: Eduard Arnold (Publishers) Ltd.

Brookes, B.C. (1971). Scientifically Speaking. An Introduction to the English of Science and Technology. Southampton: BBC.

Brumfit, Ch./Mitchell, R. (1988). Research in applied linguistics relevant to language teaching: 1987. In: language teaching, July 1988, pp 141-145.

Chambers Science and Technology Dictionary (1988). Suffolk: W & R Chambers Ltd and Cambridge University Press.

Collins Dictionary of the English Language (1981). London and Glasgow: Collins.

Collins German-English/English-German Dictionary (1981). Stuttgart: Ernst Klett Verlag.

Coulson, J.M./Richardson, S.F. (1956). Chemical Engineering, vol I, Fluid Flow, Heat Transfer and Mass Transfer. London: Pergamon Press.

Crystal, D. (1980). A First Dictionary of Linguistics and Phonetics. London: André Deutsch Limited.

Eckersley C.E./Eckersley, J.M. (1960). A Comprehensive English Grammar for Foreign Students. Hong Kong: Longman.

Fachwörterbuch Elektrotechnik-Elektronik, Englisch-Deutsch (1979). Peter-Klaus Budig (Herausgeber). Heidelberg: Dr. Alfred Hüthig Verlag

Fluck, H.-R. (1985). Fachsprachen. Einführung und Bibliographie. Tübingen: Francke Verlag.

Gerbert, M. (1970). Besonderheiten der Syntax in der technischen Fachsprache des Englischen. Halle: Max Niemeyer Verlag.

Glendinning, E.H. (1973). English in Mechanical Engineering. English in Focus. Oxford. OUP.

Glendinning, E.H. (1980). English in Electrical Engineering and Electronics. English in Focus. Oxford: OUP.

Gläser, R. (1990). Fachtextsorten im Englischen. Tübingen: Gunter Narr Verlag.

Gramley, St. (1988). Infinitive and -ing Constructions as Verb Complements. In: Bald, W.-D., Kernprobleme der englischen Grammatik - Sprachliche Fakten und ihre Vermittlung. Berlin-Schöneberg: Langenscheidt-Longman GmbH.

Halliday, M.A.K. (1988). On the language of physical science. In: Registers of Written English - Situational Factors and Linguistic Features. Mohsen Ghadessy (ed.). London and New York: Pinter Publishers.

Herbert, A.J. (1965). The Structure of Technical English. London: Longman.

Herbst, Th./Stoll, R./Westermayr, R. (1991). Terminologie der Sprachbeschreibung. Ismaning: Max Hueber Verlag.

How Things Work. The Universal Encyclopedia of Machines, (1980). Two Volumes. London: Granada Publishing Limited.

Hoffmann, L. (1976). Kommunikationsmittel Fachsprache. Eine Einführung. Berlin: Akademie Verlag.

Hoffmann, L. (1979). Towards a Theory of LSP. In: Special Language/Fachsprache 1-2, pp 12-17.

Hoffmann, L. (1987). Syntactic Aspects of LSP. In: Special Language/Fachsprache 3-4, pp 98-105.

Huckin, T./Olsen, L. (1983). English for Science and Technology. New York: McGraw Hill.

Huddleston, R. (1971). The Sentence in Written English. A Syntactic Study Based on an Analysis of Scientific Texts. Cambridge: CUP.

Huddleston, R. (1984). Introduction to the Grammar of English. Cambridge: CUP

Hudson, R.A. (1972). English Complex Sentences. An Introduction to Systemic Grammar. Amsterdam, London: North-Holland Publishing Company.

Hutchinson, T./Waters, A. (1987). English for Specific Purposes. A learning-centred approach. Musselburgh: CUP.

Kennedy, Ch./Bolitho, R. (1984). English for Specific Purposes. Hong Kong: Macmillan Publishers Ltd.

Kirsten, H. (1980). Zur Klassifizierung der ING-Formen. In: Linguistische Studien. Reihe A, Arbeitsberichte. Berlin: AdW.

Kučera, A. (1989). The Compact Dictionary of Exact Science and Technology. Volume 1, English-German. Wiesbaden: Oscar Brandstetter Verlag.

Lackstrom, J.E./Selinker, L./Trimble, L.P. (1972). Grammar and Technical English. In: English Teaching Forum X, 5.

Lamprecht, A. (1970). Grammatik der englischen Sprache. Berlin: Volk und Wissen.

Lamprecht, A. (1983). Relationale Satzanalyse. Theorie und Praxis einer konsistenten Analyse englischer Satzstrukturen. München: Max Hueber Verlag.

Leech, G. (1988). Varieties of English Grammar: The State of the Art from the Grammarian's Point of View. In: Kernprobleme der englischen Grammatik - Sprachliche Fakten und ihre Vermittlung. Berlin-Schöneberg: Langenscheidt-Longman GmbH.

Mackay, R./Mountford, A. (1987). English for Specific Purposes. London: Longman.

Matthews, R. (1987). '-ING'. In: Lehren und Lernen von Fremdsprachen im Studium. Fremdsprachen in Lehre und Forschung, Band 4. Bochum: AKS.

McDonough, J. (1984). ESP in Perspective. London and Glasgow: Collins ELT.

Meier, G. (1990). The Participle Construction of Characterization. In: Grammatical Studies in the English Language. Heidelberg: Julius Groos Verlag.

Mountford, A. (1975). English in Workshop Practice. English in Focus. Oxford: OUP.

Mullen, N.D./Brown, P.Ch. (1984). English for Computer Science. Oxford: OUP.

Nostrand van (1989). VAN NOSTRAND'S SCIENTIFIC ENCYCLOPEDIA. Seventh Edition. Two Volumes. New York.

Oxford Advanced Learner's Dictionary of Current English (1990). Fourth Edition. Oxford: OUP.

Oxford Junior Encyclopedia, Volume VIII, Engineering (1964). London: OUP.

Picket, N.A./Laster, A.A. (1984). Technical English. Writing, Reading, and Speaking. New York: Harper & Row.

Quirk, R./Greenbaum, S./Leech, G./Svartvik, J. (1985). A Comprehensive Grammar of the English Language. New York: Longman.

Richards, J./Platt, J./Weber, H. (1985). Longman Dictionary of Applied Linguistics. Hong Kong: Longman.

Sager, J.C./Dungworth, D. (1980). The Nature of Technical English. In: Wörterbuch der industriellen Technik. Band 1, Deutsch-Englisch. Wiesbaden: Oscar Brandstetter Verlag.

Sager, J.C./Dungworth, D./McDonald, P.F. (1980). English Special Languages. Wiesbaden: Oscar Brandstetter Verlag.

Sager, J.C. (1990). A Practical Course in Terminology Processing. Amsterdam/Philadelphia: John Benjamins Publishing Company.

Sinclair, J. (1990). Collins Cobuild English Grammar. London: Collins ELT.

Strevens, P. (1973). Technical, Technological, and Scientific English (TTSE). In: ELT XXVII, pp 223-234.

Swales, J. (1971). Writing Scientific English. Hong Kong: Nelson.

Swales, J. (1985). Episodes in ESP. Oxford: Pergamon Press.

Tinnefeld, Th. (1991). Überlegungen zur Schaffung einer fachsprachlichen Grammatik. In: Programm der 22. Jahrestagung der GAL vom 20. bis zum 28. September 1991 an der Johannes Gutenberg Universität Mainz. Rahmenthema: Wirtschaft und Sprache.

The New Collins Dictionary and Thesaurus (1991). Glasgow: Harper Collins Publishers.

Thomson, A.J./Martinet, A.V. (1986). A Practical English Grammar. Fourth edition. Oxford: OUP.

Trimble, L. (1985). English for Science and Technology. A discourse approach. Avon: CUP.

Wanke, J./Havliček, M. (1980). Englisch für Elektrotechniker und Elektroniker. Wiesbaden: Oscar Brandstetter Verlag.

Yates, C.St./Fitzpatrick, A. (1988). Technical English for Industry. Avon: Longman.